Invigorating
HIGH SCHOOL
Math

Invigorating
HIGH SCHOOL
Math

Practical Guidance for Long-Overdue Transformation

Steven Leinwand

Eric Milou

HEINEMANN

Portsmouth, NH

Heinemann
145 Maplewood Ave, Suite 300
Portsmouth, NH 03801
www.heinemann.com

Offices and agents throughout the world

The authors and publisher wish to thank those who have generously given permission to reprint borrowed material:

Figure 1.2, Figure A.1, Figure A.2: "Figure 2: Long Term (2023–24) Course Pathway Options" and "Table 3: Total count of core high school standards in January 2021 draft" from *2021 Oregon Draft Mathematics Standards: High School Core Mathematics*, January 2021 Draft for Public Review. Reprinted by permission of the Oregon Department of Education.

credits continue on page 203

Library of Congress Control Number: 2021910414
ISBN: 978-0-325-13416-1

Editor: Heather Anderson
Production: Victoria Merecki
Cover design: Vita Lane
Cover images (l to r): © SDI Productions/Getty Images; © Prostock-studio/ Adobe Stock; © SDI Productions/Getty Images
Interior design and typesetting: Gina Poirier, Gina Poirier Design
Manufacturing: Val Cooper

Printed in the United States of America on acid-free paper
1 2 3 4 5 VP 25 24 23 22 21
July 2021 Printing

To our incredibly supportive spouses,

Ann and Karen

Contents

Introduction

To Invigorate or to Deaden?

THE DICTIONARY IS VERY CLEAR. To *invigorate* is to give strength and energy to; to animate or give life to (www.vocabulary.com). The thesaurus is equally helpful. Under synonyms for *invigorate*, one finds *energize*, *enliven*, *jazz (up)*, *jump-start*, *pep (up)*, *stimulate*, and *vitalize* (www.thesaurus.com).

Now think of "high school mathematics." It is unlikely anyone relates it to "invigorating." Rather, high school mathematics continues to be the butt of so many jokes and horror stories. Like it or not, the reality is that high school mathematics—particularly with its current focus on precalculus algebraic skills—does *not* strengthen or energize the mind or the soul. Even our most honored high school teachers and most successful high school students would be hard-pressed to argue that traditional high school mathematics stimulates, enlivens, or vitalizes.

Instead, students, parents, and even many teachers of mathematics are far more likely to describe high school mathematics as deadening, exhausting, depressing, dull, and/or tiresome. One must turn to a long list of antonyms for *invigorating* to accurately capture how high school mathematics is typically perceived and why changes are so desperately needed.

Having dedicated much of our careers to trying to change what mathematics is taught and how it is best taught, with far too limited success, we are forced to agree with the accuracy of descriptions like *deadening* and its depressing synonyms. For most students, most of the time, the required journey from Algebra 1 to Geometry to Algebra 2, and onward to Precalculus and Trigonometry, is devoid of interest, much less excitement. It is mired in an out-of-date curriculum that not only fails to stimulate but also increasingly exacerbates inequity by closing off options and failing to prepare the vast majority of students for the realities of citizenship and work in the twenty-first century.

As we explain in the following chapters, the status quo is simply no longer acceptable. Accordingly, our intent is to provide a stimulus for discussion, complete with examples, samples, and models for serious consideration by every high school mathematics department. We begin, in Chapter 1, with a description of the challenges that high school mathematics currently faces and make the case that the status quo is obsolete and unteachable and fails to serve the overwhelming majority of our students. In Chapter 2 we review the excuses we hear for why change is so hard and so scary and why it can't be done. For each excuse we provide answers and ammunition for responding. Chapter 3 lays out the critical changes that are needed to address the challenges described in Chapter 1, creating a compendium of guiding principles or domains of invigoration that require serious consideration. We then turn, in Chapter 4, to core content for a set of common integrated courses for grades 9 and 10 and, in Chapter 5, to proposed content for a differentiated, rigorous, and coherent set of pathways for grades 11 and 12. These two chapters provide a detailed overview of the mathematics content that we believe represents both invigoration and differentiation within a set of revised and updated course offerings.

But content is only half the battle. Even updated, invigorated content will fall flat and continue to be underperforming unless it is accompanied by equivalent invigoration in our teaching, our assessments, and our use of technology. Accordingly, Chapter 6 builds on the groundbreaking work of the National Council of Teachers of Mathematics (NCTM) and summarizes the critical shifts in pedagogy that are required to effectively implement the revised curriculum and maximize accessibility to the key mathematics in the curriculum. Chapter 7 makes the case that the glue that holds everything together is the set of common, high-quality unit assessments in every course. Chapter 8 explores the ways that technology is a nonnegotiable enabler of change—both in the curriculum and in our teaching. Chapter 9 turns to modeling and explores a revised overarching purpose of high school mathematics—being adept at using mathematical skills and concepts to model and explore real-world phenomena. Chapter 10 then lays out a practical plan for implementation of these changes over a five-year period of discussion, structure building, iterative change, adjustment, and department-wide implementation. Finally, Chapter 11 includes a set of resources that exemplify many of the changes we propose and serve as a starting point for collegial discussion and implementation.

Our hope is that after reading, reviewing, and reflecting on our ideas, you will agree that the need for changing high school mathematics is imperative. We hope that you will recognize that the time for changing high school mathematics is now. Those responsible for making these changes are the high school mathematics teachers themselves, armed with compelling arguments, sensible answers to the challenges they face, and the professional support of colleagues committed to far more effectively serving the fifteen million students taking high school mathematics on any given school day in the United States. Our hope is that this book stimulates change, empowers high school mathematics teachers, and helps guide the profession on this critical journey to invigorate high school mathematics.

Part 1

Challenges, Excuses, and Guiding Principles

Before jumping from a nagging sense that there is a problem with high school mathematics directly to a set of solutions to the perceived problem, it is essential, just as in formal processes of mathematical problem solving, *to first understand the problem*. Accordingly, the three chapters in this first part of the book are designed to identify the diverse needs that are not currently being met and the challenges every high school teacher of mathematics faces. We also look at the common excuses we hear for *not* changing and propose rebuttals to these excuses. Finally, we identify and discuss a set of guiding principles that we believe must be the foundation for any plan for invigorating high school mathematics.

Another purpose of starting with challenges, excuses, and guidelines is that, as a whole, these three chapters hopefully make clear that these are not easy decisions or broadly popular changes. For nearly one hundred years the basic structure of high school mathematics has changed only a little, not because it is working so well, but because there are powerful forces with a vested interest in maintaining the status quo. Our hope is that these chapters arm everyone with the understanding and ammunition needed to take on these forces and move forward on behalf of *all* students.

As we propose in Chapter 10, on implementation, we believe that a year of study and planning is essential before any implementation is mandated. A careful and deliberative review of the ideas presented in these opening chapters can serve as a powerful starting point for discussion, consensus building, and initial planning.

1

> **Today, it seems as if nearly everyone agrees that high school mathematics needs to change. For far too long high school mathematics has not worked for far too many students.**
>
> —MATT LARSON (2016)

Challenges

Facing the Reality That High School Mathematics Is Obsolete, Is Unteachable, and Exacerbates Inequity

AS WE ENTER THE 2020s, it is essential that we acknowledge that high school math is not working for the majority of high school students. Just look at the array of challenges that we, as mathematics educators, face:

- Despite vast changes in the realities of the workplace, the expectations of knowledgeable and effective citizenship in a complex democratic society, and the ubiquitous presence of ever more powerful technology, there has been only minimal change in the content of the Algebra 1 to Geometry to Algebra 2 to Precalculus sequence of courses. Yet we know that a large body of traditional algebraic-centered high school mathematics content has very little value for most students and that everyone benefits if we eliminate what is essentially obsolete content. We also know that high school mathematics still pays too much attention to readiness for calculus and ignores the realities of how broadly important statistical understanding, data analysis, and modeling have become.

- While the Common Core State Standards for Mathematics have taken root in grades K–8 and resulted in significant changes in what and how mathematics is taught, there has been, and continues to be, a serious paucity of guidance on exactly what should now be taught in grades 9–12 mathematics. The high school curriculum remains burdened by an unteachable number of expectations that focus on breadth over depth and rote skill over modeling and application.

- While high school math remains rooted in tradition, there are significant changes taking place in the first and second years of college for which high schools must adapt.

- The current program anoints the few and leaves millions behind. The typical program effectively tracks and sorts students into a minority of students prepared for STEM careers and a majority of students left essentially underprepared for any quantitative, mathematical, or statistical future. Such programs exacerbate inequities, turn off millions to mathematics, and underserve our students and the nation.

- Finally, any cursory review of NAEP, PISA, SAT, ACT, or AP achievement data should raise concern and a rousing cry to build far more effective programs.

It is clear that the status quo is no longer acceptable and major changes in course organization, mathematical content, pedagogy, and assessment are long overdue. However, before we turn to specific guidance and justification on how this status quo must change, in this chapter we discuss the considerable challenges facing high school mathematics.

How We Got Here: A 19th-Century Framework for 21st-Century Needs

Consider the absurdity of a high school English program that includes only Shakespeare and nineteenth-century literature. No Faulkner, no Hemingway, no non-Western literature—just a lot of Dickens and Thoreau and Emily Dickinson. Or consider the bankruptcy of a high school history curriculum that stops around 1900 and conveniently ignores two world wars; the end of colonization; huge shifts in the balance of power among the United States, Russia, and China; and the history and contributions of non-Western societies. Frankly, it is too outlandish to even consider, but in many ways, high school mathematics has done just that: taken and implemented an 1894 report and made only cosmetic changes in the century and a quarter since!

Here's what the incredibly influential National Education Association's *Report of the Committee of Ten on Secondary School Studies* proposed way back in 1894 (see Figure 1.1):

- a year of algebra

- a year of algebra and concrete geometry

- a year of algebra and formal geometry

- a year of trigonometry and higher algebra.

1st Secondary School Year.		2nd Secondary School Year.	
Latin	5 p.	Latin	5 p.
English Literature, 3 p. Composition, 2 p.	5 p.	Greek	5 p.
German or French	4 p.	English Literature, 3 p. Composition, 2 p.	5 p.
Algebra	5 p.	German	4 p.
History	3 p.	French	4 p.
	22 p.	Algebra,* 2½ p. Geometry, 2½ p.	5 p.
		Astronomy (12 weeks)	5 p.
		Botany or Zoölogy	5 p.
		History	3 p.
			37½ p.
		*Option of book-keeping and commercial arithmetic.	

3rd Secondary School Year.		4th Secondary School Year.	
Latin	5 p.	Latin	5 p.
Greek	4 p.	Greek	4 p.
English Literature, 3 p. Composition, 1 p. Rhetoric, 1 p.	5 p.	English Literature, 3 p. Composition, 1 p. Grammar, 1 p.	5 p.
German	4 p.	German	4 p.
French	4 p.	French	4 p.
Algebra*	2½ p.	Trigonometry, 2 p. ½ yr. Higher Algebra, 2 p. ½ yr.	2 p.
Geometry	2½ p.	Physics	5 p.
Chemistry	5 p.	Anatomy, Physiology, and Hygiene, ½ yr.	5 p.
History	3 p.	History	3 p.
	35 p.	Geol. or Physiography, 3 p. ½ yr. Meteorology, 3 p. ½ yr.	3 p.
*Option of book-keeping and commercial arithmetic.			37½ p.

FIGURE 1.1 How Little Has Changed in Over One Hundred Years of High School Math

These recommendations were proposed when fewer than 25 percent of students graduated from high school. They emerged long before technology, in the form of calculators and computers, was available to do the lion's share of mathematical computation. And yet, how different is this algebra and geometry layer cake from what is currently experienced by millions of students? When we are honest with ourselves, the answer is "not much."

NCTM's *Catalyzing Change in High School Mathematics* (2018) puts it this way in a section understatedly titled "The Stability of High School Mathematics":

Although high school mathematics in the United States has changed in some ways over the last few decades, those changes have been relatively minor compared with the changes that society has undergone in the same period. Nevertheless, for the vast majority of students, high school mathematics continues to begin with a year of algebra followed by a year of geometry and a second year of algebra. First recommended by the Committee of Ten, this three-year pathway still identifies the courses offered by more than 90% of high schools to students in the United States. (1)

This stability ignores societal and workplace changes, underserves our students, and, bluntly, is choking the life out of mathematics.

The Common Core: A Paucity of Guidance for High School

While the grades K–8 Common Core State Standards move mathematics forward in substantive and important ways, the 9–12 Common Core standards are not adequately clear, bold, teachable, or internationally benchmarked to best serve our nation's high school students. The primary writers of the Common Core have explained, in personal conversations with the authors, that back in 2009 and 2010 they just ran out of time and, under the pressure of unreasonable deadlines, were forced to cut some corners when it came to high school. We believe that this was a serious error and that another half generation of high school students has been severely disadvantaged by the maintenance of the status quo.

The widespread acceptance and adoption of the K–8 Common Core provide important guidance on what is needed and currently missing at 9–12. The K–8 standards include

- *fewer* standards than were typically found in previous efforts

- clear examples embedded into the standards to clarify their meaning

- a focus on key concepts at each grade, wherein number and geometry now get strong emphasis early, and algebra and statistics get their appropriate due *after* quantity and shape concepts are largely established

- developmental progressions or learning trajectories that have been carefully adapted from those found in high-performing countries and present a mathematical coherence that has been sorely missing in the United States

- a shift in grade-level placement, wherein the introduction of key skills or algorithms has often been delayed by a grade, thereby providing time for building much stronger conceptual foundations for understanding *why* algorithms, like subtraction with regrouping or long division, work.

In summary, the K–8 Common Core mathematics standards are truly internationally benchmarked; are more coherent, clearer, deeper, and fewer; and thus provide powerful guidance to teachers. It is not a surprise that they are widely supported and are taking root throughout the system to the benefit of students and teachers alike.

Unfortunately, none of these positive characteristics apply to the 9–12 Common Core mathematics standards and most of their derivatives. More specifically:

- The 9–12 standards are not internationally benchmarked (no other country organizes secondary mathematics courses into Algebra 1, Geometry, and Algebra 2).

- Instead of organizing the 9–12 standards into far more sensible integrated Math 9, Math 10, and Math 11 courses, we are given aggregated standards for quantity, algebra, functions, geometry, modeling, and statistics, with many standards so broad they cross course lines.

- While the coherent learning trajectories and progressions are so clearly delineated across grades within the K–8 domains, the complete absence of progressions at 9–12 severely undermines their power and quality.

We also note that it has been more than ten years since the release of the Common Core math standards. In that decade, most states have only tinkered around the edges with minor changes to the high school standards, if any at all. Such tinkering has led to no substantial change. In fact, only since 2019 have a few states, such as Oregon, actually begun proposing significant revisions to their high school standards, and we will highlight such examples in Chapters 4 and 5.

An Array of Serious Challenges

Challenges of Content: Too Much and Not Useful Enough

Early in their first year, every beginning mathematics teacher learns that it is impossible to complete all the chapters in their assigned textbook. No one, even with an hour or more of mathematics each day, can race through fourteen or more chapters unless they practice a procedure-of-the-day, superficial treatment of mathematics, also known as instructional malpractice. Moreover, every textbook contains content that publishers include so as to offend no one, but that no one expects all teachers to include. But teachers are left asking which chapters are essential, which would be nice to complete, and which lessons and whole chapters really need to be skipped. That's not clear guidance; it's a hodgepodge of options that undermines articulation from course to course and coherence within and between courses.

Even with the knowledge that they can't cover everything, teachers are expected to squeeze 156 Common Core grades 9–12 standards into three years of instruction (although nearly 40 of them are denoted as "+ standards," with content not deemed appropriate for all students). We make little progress and serve few students when teachers are asked to teach as many as 59 standards within a single course, as proposed in the Common Core Appendix A Pathways document, resulting in more of the same racing through the curriculum with far too little mastery or understanding. Readers can Google this document, but we believe that it is so detrimental to making progress and so impossible to implement that we won't honor it with a link.

ESSENTIALLY USELESS CONTENT

Fifty years ago, students were finding square roots with pencil and paper using an arcane and quickly forgotten algorithm. Gradually, the absurdity of spending time on how to find a square root at the expense of what square roots are and why they have value, as well as the utter uselessness of this algorithm, led to its elimination from the curriculum. We challenge teachers to argue that we are *worse* off as a society with two generations completely ignorant of how to use pencil and paper to find square roots to as many decimal places as desired.

Yet halfway through a lesson on subtracting polynomials, every teacher of high school mathematics has faced the classroom reality of a student asking, "Why are we doing this?" It's a good question. So how do we respond? We either fake it, and lose credibility, with unsatisfying answers like "You'll need it next year and in Calculus!" or "It's on the SAT"—which isn't even true. Or we admit the truth and tell our students that we don't really know why we are wasting our time subtracting polynomials devoid of context or modeling or why we are adding and subtracting polynomials three months after learning about using like terms to solve equations.

The fact is, there are an overwhelming number of other current topics that raise these same questions. Some of these topics are ones that we all love. Golly gee, one of us actually loved trig identities back in the dark ages. The other one of us loved memorizing geometric theorems. But that does not give us the right to impose these essentially obsolete aspects of the curriculum on another generation of tech-savvy twenty-first-century students.

One of us had the "pleasure" of enduring the COVID-19 quarantine supervising the distance learning of Algebra 1 with a seventh grader. We spent two weeks on the drudgery of factoring and completing the square and checked every single answer in seconds with a Desmos graph or Wolfram Alpha app. If we survived the elimination of square root calculation, we can certainly survive the time-consuming menace of factoring binomials and many other topics with pencil and paper.

So start your list! There is content that every high school mathematics department can agree to ban, confident that, after open and spirited discussion, there is absolutely no downside to these decisions. We believe that such a list ought to start with such time-consuming and energy-sapping topics and procedures as

- factoring binomials

- division of polynomials and synthetic division

- trigonometric identities

- memorizing theorems

- rationalizing the denominator

- pages and pages of practice exercises without timely feedback

- using pencil and paper to solve complicated equations.

Worried about time and the messages we send to our students? Just consider how much more time we would have for conceptual understanding and a focus on applications and modeling if we modernized what currently remains an archaic curriculum for many. We will provide much more specific guidance about content in Chapters 4 and 5.

MISSING CONTENT: DATA AND STATISTICS

Mathematics teachers need look no further than the 2020 COVID-19 pandemic to recognize how seriously the traditional curriculum has failed society. The average citizen, to say nothing of the nation's leaders, is expected to understand and make decisions on the basis of data. What do these graphed trends mean? What factors explain the differences in state-by-state experiences? What can we predict? What is the impact of wearing or not wearing a mask? Did quarantining make a difference? Why must vaccines undergo a three-step testing process, what is a double-blind study, and what statistics are used to convince us that a new vaccine is safe, effective, and reliable?

In one such example, in early May 2020 the state of Georgia released a graph shown clearly showing a decline in the number of confirmed COVID-19 cases in five counties. However, a closer examination of the data on the x-axis shows the dates are not in the correct order, leading to a misleading conclusion. (To see this graph, go to your Internet search engine and search for, "Georgia's COVID-19 cases error.") Clearly, data literacy has never been more important.

For many educators, it has been both exciting and depressing to observe Governor Andrew Cuomo of New York explain the importance of R(t), the statistic used to measure the reproduction rate of a virus. He noted that we are in trouble when R(t) reaches 1.3 or higher—meaning each affected person transmits the virus to 1.3 other people—but that we can control the spread when R(t) falls below 0.9. And that when R(t) reaches 2 or 3, we get a pandemic! This cannot be the moment when eyes glaze over. It has to become the sort of knowledge that enables a government to plan effectively and its citizenry to respond wisely. This is just one example of the long-overdue need to significantly increase the time and focus on data literacy and statistical understanding in high school mathematics, and another reason to look very critically at the no-longer-useful algebraic topics mentioned earlier.

Challenges of Organization: Pathways and Tracking

A single pathway through high school mathematics ignores the diversity of mathematical needs and opportunities. When essentially 100 percent of fifth graders move to sixth grade and essentially 100 percent of eighth graders move to ninth grade, it makes sense to have a common, undifferentiated curriculum for all students. But when high school feeds students into minimum-wage jobs, the military, community colleges, technical schools, minimally competitive colleges, and highly competitive universities (including both STEM and non-STEM majors), it is absurd to have a single set of mathematics standards for a single privileged pathway. There were approximately 375,000 STEM majors out of almost 2 million college graduates in the class of 2017 (NCES 2019). That's only 19 percent of college graduates, and even when 238,000 health profession majors are added in, the expanded STEM total is *less than one-third of all college graduates.*

When a rigorous quantitative reasoning pathway and an equally rigorous statistics pathway would be so much more valuable to so many students than the traditional calculus pathway, it is time to ask why the Common Core and the majority of high school coursework still include so much precalculus content that fewer than 1 in 3 college graduates, and fewer than 1 in 5 high school graduates, are ever likely to need! We return to this need for differentiation and for diverse, but equally rigorous, pathways in Chapter 5, where we also try to debunk that argument that anything short of Algebra 2 and Precalculus is a "watered-down," less rigorous pathway.

The Insidious Practice of Tracking

As far back as 1983, the report *A Nation at Risk* included urgent language about dismantling tracking in American high schools and called for a commitment to the "twin goals of equity and high-quality schooling" (National Commission on Excellence in Education). Nearly forty years later, those goals remain unmet. In 2018, the National Council of Teachers of Mathematics published *Catalyzing Change in High School Mathematics*, which again calls for high school mathematics to discontinue the practice of tracking, including tracking students into qualitatively different or dead-end course pathways *and* tracking teachers in ways that usually ensure that the most needy students get the least experienced and weakest teachers. This publication emphatically states:

> Tracking is insidious because it places some students into qualitatively different or lower levels of a mathematics course and, in some cases, puts students into terminal mathematics course pathways that are not mathematically meaningful and do not prepare them for any continued study of fundamental mathematical

> concepts. Too often, as Stiff and Johnson (2011) attest, placement into different tracks is based on a variety of nonacademic factors, such as perceived (but not potential) academic ability, race, socioeconomic status, gender, language, or other expectations ascribed to students by adults. (NCTM 2018, 16)

The research on tracking is unequivocal: the mathematics experience of students placed in a track (or a level of a course) with less access to rigorous curriculum and high-quality instruction is qualitatively different from the mathematics experience of students not placed in such tracks (Oakes et al. 1990; Schmidt 2009; Schmidt, Cogan, and McKnight 2010/2011; Stiff and Johnson 2011; Tate and Anderson 2002). Furthermore, this difference has long-term negative effects on achievement and affective outcomes for the students in tracks with less access to rigorous and high-quality instruction, and ultimately it exacerbates learning differentials. Mathematics pathways, and the structures and practices associated with them, should be designed to eliminate tracking and both implicit and explicit bias.

Lack of Cohesion with What Comes Before and After

The Common Core, with all its positive attributes, has taken root at K–8 (as discussed above). Similarly, after years of stagnation, in the first two years of college several combined factors—a conviction that the status quo is unacceptable, new mathematics pathways that offer long-overdue alternatives to calculus, and a recent state-driven Conference Board of the Mathematical Sciences (CBMS) initiative to add pathways to high school mathematics offerings—are showing potential for important changes. In particular, we are seeing significant proliferation of alternative quantitative mathematics and statistical mathematics pathways in colleges and universities for which high school is not adequately preparing students.

In addition, researchers have found that instruction in colleges' mathematics pathways courses looks very different from instruction in colleges' standard, usually dead-end, developmental course offerings and algebra courses (Rutschow 2019). Moreover, researchers have found that students enrolled in alternative mathematics pathways courses passed college-level math at higher rates than non–math pathways students.

Any perusal of this situation quickly reveals that 9–12 is *not* adapting to be synced with K–8 and is *not* currently broadening the curriculum and course offerings to best flow into new college freshman- and sophomore-year pathways. *A Common Vision for Undergraduate Mathematical Sciences Programs in 2025* (Saxe and Braddy 2015), a bold report that summarizes recommendations from all five higher-education professional mathematics associations (see Chapter 11), calls on the community to "(1) update curricula, (2) articulate clear pathways between curricula driven by change at the K–12 level and the first courses students take in college, (3) scale up the use of evidence-based pedagogical methods, (4) find ways to remove barriers facing students at critical transition points (e.g., placement, transfer) and (5) establish stronger connections with other disciplines" (1).

More specifically, when discussing multiple pathways into and through the mathematics curriculum, the report notes that there is "a call to provide mathematically substantive options for students who are not headed to calculus," (Saxe and Braddy 2015, 13) including college-entry courses that should focus on problem solving, modeling, statistics, and applications.

The Charles A. Dana Center has led this movement at the collegiate level with the creation of math pathways, sequences of courses students take to meet the requirements of their collegiate degree programs. These pathways are designed to align with students' career and life needs and should accelerate underprepared students' entry into credit-bearing coursework. Each mathematics pathway includes rigorous, transferable, college-level content that meets the requirements of specific academic programs and careers. Increasingly, the entry-level mathematics course a student takes in college is determined by their major, rather than the conventional model of having all students move through algebra or calculus. Data from both Texas and California indicate that only about a quarter of students enrolled in public two-year institutions and about a third of graduates from public four-year institutions are in programs of study that require calculus (Burdman 2015). A growing number of students are earning degrees that, instead, require a course in quantitative reasoning or statistics.

Efforts to create new mathematics pathways in higher education that are better aligned with students' future needs, including career opportunities, provide the K–12 sector with the opportunity to reenvision high school mathematics as well. In fact, a growing number of states are examining their high school mathematics requirements. For example, the state of Oregon is capitalizing on this work with the development of high school math pathways, as shown in Figure 1.2. More details on Oregon's work can be found in the Appendix.

The Results: We Are Not Where We Want to Be

Make all the excuses you want. Question the content of the tests. Place the bulk of blame on students and their "laziness" or "lack of motivation." But a cursory review, as well as an item-by-item analysis, forces us to confront the seriousness of the gap between what students currently demonstrate and what we need them to demonstrate to have real opportunity in today's world. Below is a summary of recent student achievement data.

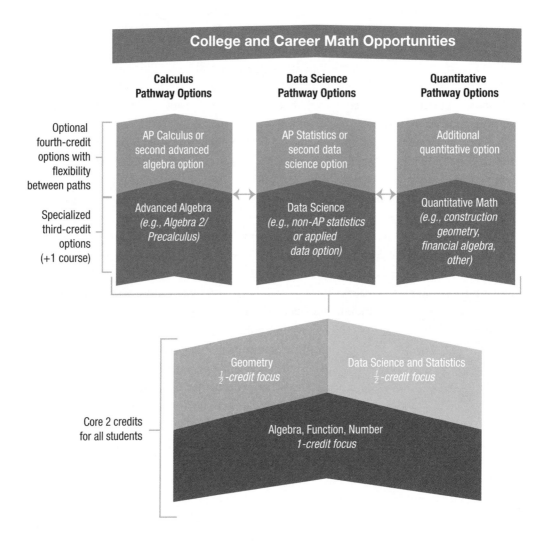

FIGURE 1.2 Oregon's Recommended High School Mathematics Options

As shown in Figure 1.3, the NAEP scores for nine-year-olds and thirteen-year-olds have risen significantly over the past thirty years, but the scores for seventeen-year-olds remain flat over this same period. It is not a pretty picture and can either depress us into inaction or motivate us to make the kinds of changes that significantly improve this student achievement data.

Similarly disturbing are the results of the Program for International Student Assessment (PISA), an international assessment of fifteen-year-old students' mathematical

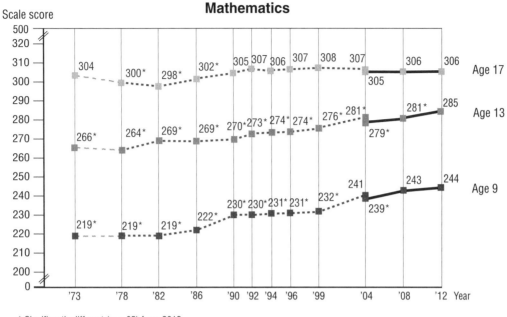

Mathematics

Scale score

* Significantly different (p < .05) from 2012.

- - - - Extrapolated data adjusting for the limited number of questions from the
1973 mathematics assessment in common with the assessments that followed

· · · · · · · Original assessment format using the same assessment procedures established for the first assessment year

——— Revised assessment format introducing more current assessment procedures and content

Source: National Center for Education Statistics (2013, 456)

FIGURE 1.3 National Assessment of Education Progress Trend Data

↙ literacy that is conducted every three years. In 2018, students in the United States performed above the Organization for Economic Cooperation and Development (OECD) average in reading (505 score points) and science (502), and below the OECD average in mathematics (478). The trend lines of the United States' mean performance in reading since 2000, mathematics since 2003, and science since 2006 are stable, with no significant improvement or decline.

Unlike most of the assessments given to students, test items on PISA are all problem-solving and application items and make our national performance rather depressing, while reinforcing our conviction that the curriculum is failing our students much more than our students are failing the test. For instance, in the United States, only 8 percent of students scored at Level 5 or higher in mathematics (OECD average: 11 percent). Six Asian countries and economies had the largest shares of students who did so: Beijing,

Shanghai, Jiangsu, and Zhejiang (China) (44 percent); Singapore (37 percent); Hong Kong (China) (29 percent); Macao (China) (28 percent); Chinese Taipei (23 percent); and Korea (21 percent). These students can model complex situations mathematically and can select, compare, and evaluate appropriate problem-solving strategies for dealing with them. U.S. students fall far short on this.

Then there are the ubiquitous and still-powerful SAT and ACT college entrance examinations taken annually by millions of high school juniors and seniors. The historical average SAT scores of college-bound seniors is shown in Figure 1.4 and has remained flat (with small ups and downs) over the past fifty years.

It should also be noted that since the first college made the SAT optional in 1969, the opt-out movement has grown steadily. Since 2013, 130 more schools have removed the requirement that students submit SATs and ACTs, bringing the total to over 1,000.

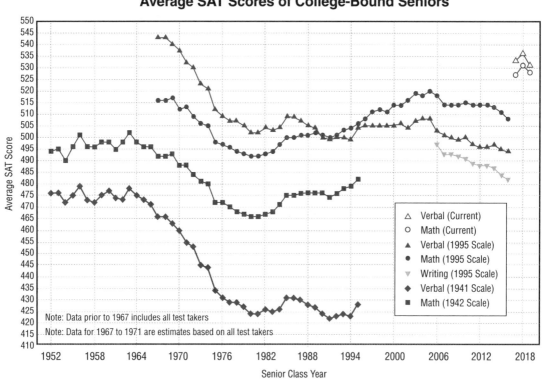

Average SAT Scores of College-Bound Seniors

Legend:
- △ Verbal (Current)
- ○ Math (Current)
- ▲ Verbal (1995 Scale)
- ● Math (1995 Scale)
- ▽ Writing (1995 Scale)
- ◆ Verbal (1941 Scale)
- ■ Math (1942 Scale)

Note: Data prior to 1967 includes all test takers
Note: Data for 1967 to 1971 are estimates based on all test takers

Sources: College Board; National Center for Education Statistics

FIGURE 1.4 Average SAT Score of College-Bound Seniors

In 2018, the University of Chicago, which admits fewer than 10 percent of applicants, became the first top-ten research university to make the test optional. And all these changes were pre-pandemic! Moreover, in May 2021, the University of California system, the largest in the country, no longer considers SAT or ACT scores in admission or scholarship decisions (Burke 2021).

We wish to draw particular attention to the raw scores—or number of items correct—that relate to particular ACT and SAT scale scores due to how often we hear, "There can't really be a problem when our school's SAT average score is 600 and ACT average score is 25." Figure 1.5 shows SAT and ACT conversion charts and reveals that students need only get 38 out of 58 items, or 66 percent, to get a 600 on the SAT and only 38 out of 60, or 63 percent, to get a 25 on the ACT! These raw scores reveal that our students can get a great many reasonable test items incorrect and still receive what is perceived as a strong score. We believe that any examination of SAT or ACT raw scores provides additional evidence of current weaknesses of today's typical high school mathematics program—even for many of our so-called "best" students.

SAT		ACT	
RAW SCORE	SCALE SCORE	RAW SCORE	SCALE SCORE
26 out of 58 items	500	31 out of 60 items	22
38 out of 58 items	600	38 out of 60 items	25
50 out of 58 items	700	46 out of 60 items	28

FIGURE 1.5 Math SAT and ACT Raw Score to Scale Score Conversion

Never have the broader aims of mathematics education been more important than they are today, when mathematics underlies so much of the fabric of society, from polling and data mining in politics, to algorithms targeting advertisements at groups of people on social media, to complex mathematical models of financial instruments, pandemics, and policies that affect the lives of millions of people. The challenges discussed in this chapter are real and remain significant obstacles to program-wide invigoration. But until we understand the extent of the problems we face, we are unlikely to be motivated to solve these problems.

In the next chapter, we'll look at the excuses we commonly hear for why these obstacles remain, and how to respond to these excuses.

Guiding Questions

1. Which of these challenges are not really challenges in your school or district? Why do you think this is the case?

2. Which of these challenges are real obstacles to change in your school or district? Why do you think this is the case? What can be done to overcome these challenges or obstacles?

3. What other challenges do you encounter that make changing so difficult? What strategies can be brought to a process of overcoming these challenges?

Don't make excuses. Make things happen.
Make changes. Then make history.

—DOUG HALL

Excuses

Why We Retain an Underperforming Status Quo

WE DON'T IGNORE the need for change because we are ignorant of the challenges described in Chapter 1. In fact, most mathematics teachers are well aware of the reality and consequences of these challenges.

We don't ignore the need to change because we don't care about our students. In fact, we care deeply about our students, but we are convinced our hands are tied and we think, "Who are we to challenge the status quo?" or "Is it worth taking on the battles that significant change would entail?" So, with the best of intentions, we make excuses. We find reasons *not* to change and we excuse away a clearly underperforming status quo.

Let's look at these excuses—some strong, some excruciatingly weak.

Excuses About Students

They don't have basic skills.

Everywhere we work we hear, "How can we do anything different when so many of our students have such extraordinary gaps in skills?" When we probe, we are told about ninth graders who don't know their multiplication facts, who can't do long division, and who are lost with anything involving fractions. We too have encountered students like this and recognize how frustrating it is to be responsible for teaching algebra to students with these missing pieces.

However, in most schools we are talking about no more than 20 percent of the students with deficiencies of this magnitude. Given that 20 percent of our students, on average, perform at an advanced level, we argue that this leaves the middle 60 percent, for whom this excuse is inappropriately applied. It is not because of skill gaps that this middle 60 percent are not learning enough; it is more likely because the mathematics they are being taught and how it is being taught just do not meet their intellectual or emotional needs. As we describe later, there is definitely a need for intensive interventions in the form of double-period boost-up courses for the weakest 20 percent, but that leaves a large proportion of our students who ought to be able to succeed given opportunity, experience, and effort.

Our experience is that nearly all single-digit number fact problems come down to issues with 6×7, 6×8, 6×9, 7×7, 7×8, 7×9, 8×8, 8×9, and 9×9. That is, lingering memory problems involve only nine fact families for which students need accessible strategies to replace the lack of memorization. Similarly, who really still does long division with paper and pencil or complicated fraction problems? The free, accessible calculator on our smartphones takes care of this issue in the real world but remains an obstacle only in schools where such technology is, unfortunately, often banned from classrooms.

Moreover, we agree that lack of fraction understanding is a common challenge for students moving into high school, as shown in research:

- The National Assessment of Educational Progress (NAEP) found that 50 percent of eighth graders could not correctly order the magnitudes of three fractions ($\frac{2}{7}$, $\frac{1}{12}$, and $\frac{5}{9}$).

- When asked whether .274 or .83 was larger, most fifth and sixth graders chose .274 (Rittle-Johnson, Siegler, and Alibali 2001).

- The difficulty extends to adolescents and adults; fewer than 30 percent of U.S. eleventh graders translated .029 into the correct fraction, and community college students showed similar weaknesses (Kloosterman 2010).

We acknowledge this problem but we also know the solution. We know that the teaching of fractions in the United States is overwhelmingly focused on understanding fractions as parts of a whole, using area models and pie charts, and teaching students the procedures for adding or multiplying. In contrast, we know that the focus should be on the measurement interpretation of fractions—how they fall on a number line, the relationships between numbers that are represented by a fraction, and the use of fractions in contextual situations. This conceptual and contextual approach uses number sense to build deeper understanding, and it is the same approach that can lead to better results in high school.

In the final analysis, we believe that the two overarching, nonnegotiable basic skills that enable success in high school mathematics are the abilities to answer these questions:

- Given a problem situation, how can I use *number sense* to estimate the answer before performing the calculation or using technology?

- Given a problem situation with data, do I press the +, –, ×, or ÷ key to get a useful quantitative result?

These are the true basic skills that need to be reinforced at every stage of mathematical learning and that more than adequately enable students to succeed in invigorated high school mathematics.

They just aren't motivated.

That's right! If we are honest with ourselves, most high school students, unless they are abnormal geeks (like the authors), have little reason to be motivated by the majority of high school algebraic-centered mathematics. Look at the endless parade of mindless worksheets with nary an application nor a reason for students to feel the need to learn these skills. Look at the non-answers from teachers they get when they ask, "Why do we need to learn this?" Look at how we tend to allocate four days to skills, many of which can be done with technology, appropriate apps, or Google, and then squeeze in one day of fake applications, often with absurd data.

Not convinced? Consider how many lessons and days we allocate to solving linear equations before our students ever need to *create* an equation and then solve it in a meaningful context. Where does this approach generate motivation? Instead, it reinforces a mindset of "just tell me what to do to get the right answer." Instead, we could easily launch the functions unit with the story of getting a speeding ticket in Vermont, where, not that long ago, the fine was $4 for every mile over the 65-mph speed limit plus a $10 processing fee. We ask what students notice and how they can understand and represent this situation. We convert the words to a graph and identify where the 4, the 65, and the 10 appear in the graph. We ask what the driver and the police officer might be interested in knowing. We then relate the speed to the fine and unleash students to find such things as the fine when you were going 86 miles per hour or the speed you must have been going if your fine was $74. We add a constraint that the maximum fine is $200 and ask about the speed at which it no longer matters. We change to another state with different parameters and explore and compare the tables and graphs that emerge. With realistic examples like this, motivation is rarely an issue with nearly all high school students.

Excuses About Future Needs

I've got to prepare them for the tests.

There is no question that tests like the SAT, the ACT, and the AP exams exert extraordinary pressure. We fear to deviate in any way that might jeopardize our students' opportunity to succeed on these exams. However, as we saw in Chapter 1, we are not now adequately preparing students for these tests, and in fact, teach a lot of content that never appears on these exams.

Our advice is, before moaning and groaning about these tests, every high school teacher of mathematics should go online and take a sample SAT or ACT examination (https://collegereadiness.collegeboard.org/sat/practice/full-length-practice-tests and https://www.act.org/content/act/en/products-and-services/the-act/test-preparation/free-act-test-prep.html) and link the test items with what you teach and what you don't teach or emphasize. Look at the content you currently teach that is nowhere found on these tests. Then examine the tested content that is only skimmed over in your classes at best. Then look at the thinking and reasoning—more than procedural knowledge—required by many of the test items and that are not typically reflected in our instruction. We urge teachers to embed selected sample and released items as part of daily cumulative review practice, homework, and unit assessments. We also note the growing list of over one thousand schools that are SAT-optional, including some of the highest-ranked schools in the United States, such as

- Bates College
- Bowdoin College
- Bryn Mawr College
- George Washington University
- Hofstra University
- Sarah Lawrence College
- Smith College
- University of Chicago
- Wake Forest University
- Wesleyan University.

Moreover, a study released in early 2020 of over fifty-five thousand students who graduated from Chicago public schools and immediately attended a four-year college showed that high school grade point averages predict college graduation rates five times more accurately than ACT scores (Allensworth and Clark 2020).

It *is* important to note the debilitating impact of Part 1 of the Advanced Placement AB Calculus examination, that is, the pencil-and-paper multiple-choice items—and its impact on what and how we teach. Unfortunately, the demand in Part 1 for paper-and-pencil facility with memorized procedures to find derivatives and integrals is how and why we justify so much of what we continue to teach. But why use the excuse of even this test when only a small percentage of our students ever take an AP Calculus exam? Moreover, we think of AP Calculus as the penultimate achievement of high school mathematics but conveniently ignore the international standard of the eleventh- and twelfth-grade International Baccalaureate, for which all students have a thirty-two-page study guide with all the formulas needed and are allowed to access the guide while taking the IB assessments!

But it's what the colleges demand.

Many postsecondary institutions around the country have engaged in serious efforts to reform their math requirements, as highlighted in Chapter 1. Colleges are now offering new pathways in areas like statistics and quantitative reasoning for students with interests outside the STEM disciplines, which are served by traditional math pathways, and de-emphasizing remedial math tests and courses in favor of corequisites and other just-in-time approaches. These postsecondary reforms have paved the way for reconsidering the mathematics required for college admission, as well as the mathematical preparation high schools provide. It is time for high schools to develop pathway options that much more appropriately prepare students for a postsecondary world that branches into a broad spectrum of careers for which calculus is not needed. In fact, the data are clear: only a small proportion of high school students will use algebraic-centered mathematics in college or in their careers (see Figure 2.1).

Proportion of associate degree graduates in STEM fields	8%
Proportion of BA holders using Algebra 2 or beyond	18% to 31%
Proportion of bachelor's degree graduates in STEM fields	19%
Number of community college programs that required Algebra 2 mastery of entering students	1 out of 441

Sources: Daro and Asturias (2019); NCES (2019); NCEE (2013); Georgetown University Center on Education and the Workforce (2013)

FIGURE 2.1

The fact that all math courses have traditionally led to calculus shows the influence that college admissions systems have on high school pathways. Often, university admissions offices use calculus as an indicator of achievement. This emphasis in the high school curriculum creates two problems: First, not all students are interested in fields that require calculus. Second, students must accelerate through a specific sequence of courses in order to reach calculus. The pressure to take calculus creates pressure on students to accelerate, thereby skipping other valuable mathematics content or compressing the time spent on each topic. It means rushing through one of the highest priorities in high school mathematics, which is developing conceptual understanding of mathematics. Figure 2.2 shows that only 20 percent of two-year college students enroll in programs of study that require calculus and only 28 percent of four-year college students enroll in programs of study that require calculus (Burdman 2015).

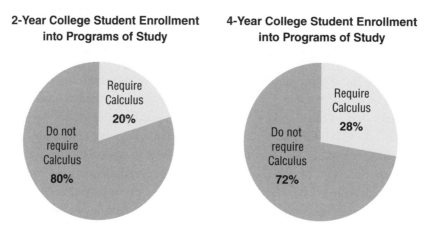

FIGURE 2.2

Moreover, David Bressoud (2015), former president of the Mathematical Association of America (MAA), argues about high school calculus:

> First, just because students can succeed in calculus in the supportive environment of a high school does not guarantee that they will be successful when they get to college. The most useful skill for success in college is the ability to learn on one's own, to be able to think critically about what one reads or views in videos, and to use this critical analysis to build a personal, coherent, and functional mental structure for the many concepts of calculus. Getting students successfully through a test, even an AP Calculus exam, is by itself no guarantee that they will be successful in college. Second, a calculus experience in high school that does not rise

to the level of being able to earn a 3 or higher on an AP Calculus exam does not
seem to have any effect, positive or negative, on performance in Calculus 1 when
the student gets to college. This finding draws into question much of the rush
to calculus in high school. It has become a cliché in U.S. colleges and universities
that students fail calculus not because they do not understand calculus; they
fail it because they have not mastered precalculus. An alternative to calculus in
high school that focuses on strengthening students' understanding of algebra,
geometry, trigonometry, and functional relations while building problem solving
skills would be very welcome. (184–85)

   In addition, fifty years ago virtually every mathematics problem in practice was
continuous and deterministic. Problems with a discrete or stochastic component were
almost nonexistent. Basically, algebraic methods and differential equations ruled. Today
the tables have turned 180 degrees as virtually every problem that arises is inherently
discrete (in large part because of technology) and virtually every problem has some
probabilistic component (there is always some uncertainty). But the mathematics curriculum, especially its first few years, has not changed to reflect the needs of the people
who use mathematics today. There are still schools where college algebra requirements
force large numbers of students (who do not need much in the way of such skills for
their majors) into college algebra–related courses (Gordon 2008). This needs to change.
   However, there is some positive news on the collegiate front. In the response to
the call to modernize college mathematics content, some in higher education have
developed and implemented multiple mathematics pathways that offer differentiated,
rigorous mathematics courses tailored to students' academic and career goals. Similarly,
some higher-education institutions are implementing a corequisite model that enables
students to immediately enter college-credit-bearing courses with support from corequisite courses that help students effectively engage with college-level coursework. The
preliminary research shows that such corequisite course models are seeing double and
triple the number of students passing their first college-level mathematics course, and
in half the time or less (Charles A. Dana Center 2018).

Excuses Related to Our Systems

There just isn't enough time.

Correct! Unless you have a locked-in minimum of 60 minutes per day for each of four
years of high school mathematics, you and your students are being set up! The standard
45- or 47-minute (or even 42-minute) period per day or the 90-minute block every

other day do *not* provide the time needed to accomplish what we are being asked to do. When we hear complaints about what the high school mathematics department *isn't* accomplishing and are told that the teachers have a 45-minute period for math each day, we have already identified a major reason for the achievement problems. Of course, how the time is spent is more important than simply the amount of time, but when great teachers are asked to "cover a curriculum," "raise test scores," and "meet standards for all students," anything less than 60 minutes per day makes this nearly impossible.

My textbook guides what I do.

An effective mathematics curriculum is driven by a coherent set of standards or expectations. The curriculum is only supported, not driven, by instructional materials. As discussed in the previous chapter, no one, even with one hour of mathematics each day, can race through fourteen or more chapters unless they practice a procedure-of-the-day, superficial treatment of mathematics. The standards, and unit assessments that are aligned with those standards, should guide what we do. Abrogating that responsibility to textbooks is not professional and doesn't serve our students.

I don't have the technology I need to do things differently.

When our smartphones—ubiquitous devices in the hands of more than 90 percent of high school students—have free calculators and access to free apps and sites such as Desmos (which is now allowed on the IB exam, the NWEA MAP, the Smarter Balanced assessment, and more than twenty-five state tests; see www.desmos.com/testing), then access to technology essentially stops being a problem. What teenager doesn't have access to a smartphone today? At worst, two students can easily share a smartphone when necessary. In other words, if we work around destructive cell phone bans, appropriate technology is readily available for nearly *all* students. This situation allows us to finally work around any problems of access to expensive handheld calculators or different kinds of calculators.

This situation also means that we have no excuses *not* to expect access to and use of powerful technology in our classrooms and on our tests. We should not limit access to smartphones because a few students might abuse them; instead, this is a classroom management issue that can and must be solved. Restricting these devices because they can disrupt and distract suggests that the mathematics being taught needs to be far more relevant and motivating. Many companies have developed test modes that will prevent other applications on the phone, including the camera, from being used during class. We will have much more to say on this in Chapter 8.

I don't have the training.

This is an entirely legitimate excuse, albeit a highly problematic one. Teachers cannot do what they can't envision or don't understand. Moreover, teachers need collaborative structures such as course committees and collegial visits to share ideas and give and get feedback. Professional isolation remains the single greatest obstacle to the quality and improvement of instruction. So, rather than use the lack of training as an excuse, we hope it becomes an opportunity for changing the professional culture in which we work. We return to this important aspect of our work in Chapter 10, on implementation.

Guiding Questions

1. Which excuses are most familiar to you?

2. Which excuses apply to your school or district?

3. What other excuses for not changing do you have or encounter?

4. How can we respond in a practical, reasoned way to the excuses we hear or make, so that the excuses don't become obstacles to change?

3

Change is the law of life, and those who
look only to the past and present
are certain to miss the future.

—JOHN F. KENNEDY (1963)

Guiding Principles

Domains of Invigoration

THIS CHAPTER INTRODUCES fourteen guiding principles or domains of invigoration that require serious consideration, discussion, planning, and, when appropriate,
implementation. These domains, summarized in Figure 3.1, arise from the challenges we
have already delineated and from our experiences in high schools and with mathematics
teachers across the country.

Goals and Purposes

GUIDING PRINCIPLE

*The high school mathematics program must have a shared, written, and honored
set of goals and purposes that guide decision-making, policy, and program.
These living principles must address the unique role of mathematics in our
society and the critical need for mathematical literacy on the part of all students.
They must include such purposes as understanding and critiquing the world;
experiencing wonder, joy, and beauty; and expanding professional opportunity,
instead of merely preparing students for the next course and for required college
entrance examinations.*

DOMAINS OF INVIGORATION FOR HIGH SCHOOL MATHEMATICS

DOMAIN/ PRINCIPLE	SUMMARY	CHAPTERS WHERE ELABORATED
GOALS AND PURPOSES	The high school mathematics program must have a shared, written, and honored set of goals and purposes that guide decision-making, policy, and program.	Chapter 3
VISION	The high school mathematics program must be guided by a descriptive and explicit vision of effective teaching and learning of mathematics.	Chapter 3
EQUITY AND ACCESS	The high school mathematics program must ensure that all students have access to a high-quality mathematics curriculum and high-quality instruction.	Chapter 6
CULTURE	The high school mathematics program must operate within a culture of mutual respect, honoring the dignity of all, and collegial collaboration between and among the adults and the students.	Chapter 6
SCOPE	The high school mathematics program must focus on the essential ideas and processes of mathematics.	Chapters 4 and 5
DIFFERENTIATION	The high school mathematics program must be built around a common core of essential and important mathematics differentiated by life and career goals.	Chapters 5 and 6
INTEGRATED MATHEMATICS	The high school mathematics program must recognize that mathematics is a unified body of knowledge about quantity, change, uncertainty, shape, and dimension.	Chapters 4 and 5
CONTENT AND PROCESS STANDARDS	The high school mathematics program must be driven by standards or expectations that delineate the learning goals for each course and each unit within each course.	Chapters 4, 5, and 6
CONNECTIONS	The high school mathematics program must include explicit and coherent exploration of how one piece of mathematics relates to other pieces of mathematics.	Chapters 4, 5, and 6

FIGURE 3.1   *continues*

DOMAINS OF INVIGORATION FOR HIGH SCHOOL MATHEMATICS, *cont.*

DOMAIN/ PRINCIPLE	SUMMARY	CHAPTERS WHERE ELABORATED
CONTEXT AND MODELING	The high school mathematics program must include situations, applications, and contemporary problems, often interdisciplinary in nature, that illustrate the usefulness of mathematics.	Chapter 9
ASSESSMENT	The high school mathematics program must recognize assessment as an integral part of instruction.	Chapter 7
TECHNOLOGY	The high school mathematics program must make full use of technologies that increase the productivity of instruction and enrich students' experiences.	Chapter 8
ADEQUATE TIME	The high school mathematics program must have adequate time to effectively meet the learning standards and implement the vision of teaching and learning that guides our work.	Chapter 10
PROFESSIONAL GROWTH AND COLLABORATION	The high school mathematics program must be supported by intensive attention to ongoing professional growth and collaboration among the mathematics teachers.	Chapter 10

FIGURE 3.1, *continued*

Without clarity of goals and purposes, we meander, we invite incoherence and conflict, and we underserve. Consider the importance of a clear, stated learning goal for each lesson. With such a goal in mind, we are better able to identify prerequisite knowledge, select appropriate tasks, ask the right questions, and construct the right formative assessment exit ticket. Conversely, without pausing to clarify a lesson goal, too often we end up punting—showing, telling, and providing opportunities to practice instead of teaching for depth and broader purposes.

The same holds true for a mathematics department. We believe that change begins with discussions that address the questions "What are the specific goals of four years of mathematics courses?" and "What are the purposes of learning mathematics in our high school?"

In *Catalyzing Change in High School Mathematics*, the National Council of Teachers of Mathematics (NCTM) urges us to consider a three-part purpose of school mathematics that includes expanding professional opportunity, understanding and critiquing the world, and experiencing wonder, joy, and beauty (2018, 9–12). The implications of this shift in purpose are significant. To expand professional opportunity, high school mathematics must fully consider the diverse future plans and accompanying mathematical needs of students. For students to better understand and critique the world, high school mathematics must ensure that mathematical experiences get connected to situations, problems, and phenomena of interest. And to ensure that students experience wonder, joy, and beauty in lieu of drudgery and pain, high school mathematics must be infused with tasks and questions and projects that bring out that wonder and beauty. One of our goals throughout this book is to describe and exemplify these broader purposes of high school mathematics.

Here is a sample statement of goals and purposes that we hope can be used to start discussions, make revisions, and eventually build consensus on the development of a goal statement that you and your colleagues can use and live by:

The overarching purpose of the High School Mathematics Department is to mathematically empower every student over the course of four years of relevant, applicable, and appropriate mathematics coursework. Our efforts to achieve this ambitious purpose, as advocated by the National Council of Teachers of Mathematics, are guided by our desire to provide all students with the opportunity to develop competence in using mathematics to understand and critique the world and its social and natural phenomena; ensure that all students experience wonder, joy, and beauty when learning mathematics; and expand all students' career opportunities after high school.

Accordingly, the overarching goals of the High School Mathematics Department are to

- provide a meaningful and engaging program of studies, including a common integrated essential core followed by differentiated pathways to prepare all students for college and the world of work

- implement instructional practices and department policies that provide equitable access to important mathematics for all students

- ensure that in every class students are expected to ask penetrating questions, explain their thinking, make reasonable estimates and predictions, and justify and respond to one another's mathematical arguments, strategies, and decisions

- ensure that all mathematical skills and concepts are taught within a context of reasoning, problem solving, and mathematical modeling.

This statement provides a broad, clear statement of purpose that explains why we are doing what we do and a short set of goals that define, in specific terms, how we plan to accomplish this purpose. We envision such a revised and broadened statement of goals and purposes being front and center on the department's web page, in the mathematics department section of the course catalog, and in poster form in every classroom where mathematics is taught.

In another school, the mathematics department was challenged to create a definition of a world-class mathematics program as an aspirational statement with which to periodically assess the overall quality of K–12 mathematics. Here is what the teachers drafted:

World-Class Mathematics at Jefferson High School: A Shared, Written Definition of Excellence

As it pertains to Jefferson High School, our mathematics program

- blends systematically the development of a strong foundation of mathematical skills, conceptual understanding and applications, and the valuing of academic success, found in the highest-performing East Asian countries, with the focus on problem solving, investigation, reasoning, justification, and modeling, found in the most successful Western approaches, to create an empowering intercultural mathematics program

- provides coherent alignment of a shared vision, progressions of learning objectives, curriculum materials, instructional practices and assessments, and differentiated approaches of teaching strategies and student learning support—with each of these components thoughtfully implemented and revised based on accepted research findings and student performance data

- ensures that all students experience the beauty, awe, and joy of mathematics; develop curiosity, perseverance, self-confidence, and the ability to argue and justify mathematically; and build number sense, symbol sense, spatial sense, and data sense throughout their mathematical experiences, as parts of a mathematics tool kit that gets expanded and refined each year

- pledges, through collaborative structures and intentional professional growth opportunities, that all teachers will have the time, technological tools, resources, and support to effectively implement the program with high levels of effectiveness

- builds a schoolwide culture, including students, teachers, administrators, and parents, that values mathematics, sees the value of a world-class mathematics program that addresses the needs and demands of our ever-changing world, and supports this shared vision of a world-class program

- confirms, through differentiated approaches to teaching and learning in every mathematics classroom, and targeted resources, that high levels of mathematical skill and understanding are achieved by each and every student.

It is easy to draft fancy and flowery language. There is a long history of ignoring such words and filing away these lofty statements of goals and purposes. Our hope is that these two sample statements serve as initial thought provokers to help stimulate discussion and drafting of statements that work for you and your colleagues.

Questions to Ask Yourselves

- Where in your stated goals or purpose statement is there reference to effective citizenship or to the demands of preparation for a changing world?

- Where in your stated goals or mission are there references to the fundamental purposes of learning mathematics?

- Where in your stated goals or mission is there reference to common essential content for all and differentiated pathways to meet different individual aspirations?

Vision

GUIDING PRINCIPLE

The high school mathematics program must be guided by a descriptive and explicit vision of effective teaching and learning of mathematics—a statement that conveys classroom norms and expectations for professional behavior on the part of students, teachers, and administrators. Effective vision statements support the implementation of the goals and purposes of the program through consistent use of research-affirmed pedagogical practices.

While a statement of goals and purposes frames a large view of what we do and serves as a message to all stakeholders, a teaching and learning vision statement is where we share among ourselves exactly what we should and should not be seeing in classrooms where mathematics is being taught. It defines expectations for professional behavior. In an invigorated high school mathematics department, a shared vision statement—when widely bought into and used—guides pedagogical decision-making, coaching and supervision support, and even teacher evaluation.

We draw from NCTM's eight mathematics teaching practices as defined and described in *Principles to Actions* (2014) to help us craft a vision of what these practices look like in mathematics classrooms. Here is one straightforward vision statement for consideration:

Our vision of effective teaching and learning of mathematics is based on our understanding of what common sense, the wisdom of practice, and research tell us about maximizing learning in our classroom. At our high school, when mathematics is being taught, planning will ensure, implementation will establish, and observation will confirm the following:

- clear statements and brief discussion of lesson goals, instead of "Today we are doing Lesson 4.5 or pages 214–217"
- use of context whenever appropriate, instead of just naked numbers
- use of rich tasks, instead of just worksheets of exercises
- focused oral *and* written questions, instead of just making things up as we go along
- frequent opportunities for, and expectations of, student discourse, instead of just telling
- gradual reveal of tasks, problems, and solutions, instead of just dumping whole paragraphs
- consistent use of multiple representations, instead of just numeric or symbolic representations
- consistent seeking and presenting of alternative approaches, instead of just providing one way to get an answer
- clear expectations for explanations and justifications, instead of just focusing on correct answers
- valuing common errors and misconceptions, instead of just a search for right answers

- consistent expectations that the mathematics will make sense as students construct understanding, instead of just lecturing, showing, and practicing

- gathering and reviewing evidence of learning or the lack thereof, instead of just "I taught it and let the chips fall where they may."

Here is an alternative model adapted from a network of charter schools:

A Guiding Vision for Inquiry-Based, Conceptually Driven, Sense-Making Mathematics in Every Mathematics Class Every Day

If our shared commitment is that every Washington High School student receives well-planned, well-executed mathematics instruction that consistently reflects our vision of active engagement in thought-provoking tasks, productive discussion about mathematical ideas and common misconceptions, and the individual and collective construction of understanding via problem solving and inquiry,

THEN this commitment requires that teachers plan their lessons around **rich tasks** that are supported by **targeted questions** and powerful **lesson debrief discussions**. Such lessons are diametrically opposite to the "I show, we practice, you do" model of direct instruction that essentially tells students what to remember and how to get right answers. For example, the "trick" to "invert and multiply" (as opposed to understanding that dividing by a number is the same as multiplying by the reciprocal of that number) works in the short term, but does not support mathematics as a sense-making enterprise and does not foster an inherent love of mathematics and its power and beauty.

MOREOVER, the problem we face as a community of teachers, administrators, and parents is that our vision is **not** widely shared, **not** fully understood or even believed, **not** consistently supported, and therefore **not** consistently implemented for all students every day. To begin to address this problem, the chart below [Figure 3.2] summarizes what students, teachers, and leaders are, and are not, doing to make inquiry-based, conceptually driven, sense-making mathematics the norm in every Washington High School mathematics class.

WHAT **STUDENTS** ***ARE*** DOING	WHAT **TEACHERS** ***ARE*** DOING	WHAT **LEADERS** ***ARE*** DOING
▪ Actively engaging in solving rich problems that are aligned with the curriculum standards ▪ Regularly engaging in productive discourse about their thinking and reasoning ▪ Grappling with mathematical ideas and making and exploring conjectures about those mathematical ideas	▪ Thoroughly studying the curriculum standards, the textbook, and other resources to develop an understanding of the key mathematical understandings across a grade, unit, or lesson ▪ Carefully selecting rich tasks that support reasoning and problem solving ▪ Anticipating students' solutions and strategies for each task ▪ Carefully crafting and asking targeted questions that focus on the key mathematical understandings ▪ Making frequent use of the critical questions "Why?" "Can you explain?" "Who did it differently?" "Can you convince the class?" and "How did you picture that?" ▪ Regularly collecting and using formal and informal evidence to assess scholar understanding of the big mathematical ideas and adjusting their instruction accordingly	▪ Regularly meeting with teachers to help them think through their lesson plans, including clarifying the learning goal and selecting rich, aligned tasks and the questions to be asked during the lesson ▪ Co-teaching the lesson in ways that support the teacher and maintain a focus on the learning goals ▪ Taking notes to support a productive debriefing and action-planning session
WHAT **STUDENTS** ***ARE NOT*** DOING	WHAT **TEACHERS** ***ARE NOT*** DOING	WHAT **LEADERS** ***ARE NOT*** DOING
▪ Solving more than three naked problems from a worksheet without the chance to explain their thinking ▪ Listening to explanations by the teacher without interruption ▪ Regurgitating procedures to get answers	▪ Showing students how to solve problems and expecting them to replicate the process solely on the basis of remembering ▪ Using the phrase "this is the rule" or "this is how you solve this" or "this is what you have to remember" without including reasons, explanations, or a focus on why ▪ Allowing students to solve problems without providing any opportunities for feedback	▪ Sitting on the sidelines, without interrupting or participating in the lesson ▪ Using the co-teaching and coaching process only for evaluation ▪ Using only co-teaching and coaching, without providing opportunities for preplanning and debriefing

FIGURE 3.2

In creating these statements, like all great teachers, we borrow and steal from other for initial drafts and then collaboratively and iteratively craft statements upon which the entire department can agree. Often the process is as important as the final product as we grapple with building consensus around our professional expectations for ourselves and our colleagues.

Questions to Ask Yourselves

- Does your department have a vision statement that describes what should be happening in effective mathematics classrooms? If not, why?
- What might be the benefits of collaboratively developing such a statement?
- What's to stop you from starting with the above examples and collaboratively creating a vision statement for your high school mathematics department that works for you and your colleagues?

Equity and Access

GUIDING PRINCIPLE
The high school mathematics program must ensure that all students have access to a high-quality mathematics curriculum and high-quality instruction. The program sets high, but reasonable, expectations and provides the support and resources needed to ensure that these expectations are attainable by all students.

It is a sad but all too common reality that school mathematics, particularly high school mathematics, acts as a filter, limiting access and denying opportunities for many students, often with the best of motives. When some students get the best teachers, have consistent access to technology, and embrace a curriculum that opens doors, while two doors down the hall or in the school down the street, other students get the least experienced teachers, have a primarily pencil-and-paper skill-based program, and endure a curriculum that is essentially a dead end, there is a serious problem.

In too many cases and places, high school mathematics continues to be a powerfully effective sorting machine, ensuring that far too many students leave high school woefully unprepared for the world of postsecondary education and work despite having taken three or four years of high school mathematics. In our experiences, in too many schools and districts this situation emerges from a conspiracy of well-meaning teachers, misguided counselors, and, too often, upper-middle-class parents concerned only about maintaining the relative privilege of their children.

To rectify this severely inequitable situation, we turn to NCTM's *Principles to Actions* (2014) and focus on the core "productive belief" that "mathematics ability is a function of opportunity, experience and effort—not of innate intelligence. Mathematics teaching and learning cultivate mathematics abilities. All students are capable of participating and achieving in mathematics, and all deserve support to achieve at the highest levels" (63).

How different this "productive belief" is from the far more common and insidious unproductive belief that "students possess different innate levels of ability in mathematics, and these cannot be changed by instruction. Certain groups or individuals have it while others do not" (63). Until beliefs like this are banished from our profession, high school mathematics will never be invigorating or designed in ways that truly serve all students.

But what specific actions ensure "opportunity, experience and effort?" We begin by advocating for the equitable teaching practices enumerated in NCTM's *Catalyzing Change in High School Mathematics* (2018, 32–34) and discussed in greater detail in Chapter 6. Access and equity begin with our instructional practices and the array of behaviors that enable all students to feel socially, emotionally, and intellectually safe and valued in every classroom. Too often we have hidden behind the excuse that we teach *mathematical content* to students and, if it doesn't work, the problem is most often the student. We need to recognize that our job is to teach *students* mathematics and that their feelings of safety, belonging, and being valued as people and learners ultimately determine how much they will learn and succeed.

In addition, we implement the vision of this guiding principle—providing opportunity and experiences—when we have a system of retesting for every unit assessment to provide second chances (more in Chapter 7), and when we replace the pernicious system of tracking with a much fairer system of selective acceleration and differentiated enrichment, as described in Chapters 4 and 5.

Questions to Ask Yourselves

- In what ways does your high school mathematics department provide access and equity to the students in your school?

- In what ways, when you are honest with yourselves, do you recognize that your high school mathematics department fails to maximize access and equitable opportunity to all students?

- How can you justify a system of tracks in high school mathematics that anoints some for a future of success and relegates others to a future with very limited opportunities?

- What specific shifts in practice and policy do you believe will significantly enhance access and equitable opportunity for the students in your school?

Culture

GUIDING PRINCIPLE

The high school mathematics program must operate within a culture of mutual respect, honoring the dignity of all, and collegial collaboration between and among the adults and the students in which the empowerment of both teachers and students drives what we do and how we do it. Even when goals and purpose statements, along with vision statements and policies to ensure equity and access, are in existence, they are only as meaningful as their implementation in the form of a shared culture that pervades how the mathematics department operates.

It is a truism of all organizations that "culture eats strategy for breakfast"—a phrase attributed to management guru Peter Drucker. However, few high school mathematics departments spend much time thinking about the culture in which they operate and which they wittingly and unwittingly communicate through actions every minute of every day.

In this case, adapting a definition from online dictionaries is helpful because mathematics department culture is generally not a topic of much discussion:

> A culture consists of the shared customary beliefs, social norms, and typical behaviors or habits of a particular social group. Culture is the set of shared attitudes, values, goals, and practices that characterizes an organization or group.

> Humans acquire culture through the processes of enculturation and socialization in which cultural norms codify acceptable conduct and guide behavior, language, and demeanor—thereby serving as a template for expectations within a social group.

In an invigorated, effective, and equitable mathematics department and program, there is a tangible sense of *belonging* and being *valued*. These characteristics define the culture. Students are never put down or made to feel dumb. Instead, they are welcomed into a mathematics learning community, their thinking is celebrated, their mistakes are seen as learning opportunities, and they know they are in an intellectually and emotionally safe place. In short, regardless of their ability, the mathematics classroom is felt to be a place where they belong and can thrive.

And it is easy to see and feel the ambient culture in classrooms. Just imagine randomly walking into three or four mathematics classrooms in your high school on any given morning. Are the desks all in rows in every room, or are students, and their desks or tables, organized in pairs, trios, or quartets, or is it some of each from room to room? How about what the students are doing? Are they actively engaged, working together, and using technology to solve what appear to be engaging tasks, or are they sitting compliantly listening to the teacher lecture, or do you see some of each? What's on the walls? Is the lesson goal clear and posted? Is an interactive whiteboard being used, or do you see effective use of animated slides on a screen, or is everything still being done with markers on a whiteboard by the teacher in the front of the room? Do you see similar approaches and problems in each algebra or geometry class, or does it look like students with two different teachers are in two different schools? How is homework reviewed? Does it count toward a grade? Is "going over homework" just a recitation of right answers? Are there ever other teachers or other adults in any of the classes you observe? What are they doing to support teaching and learning? And what about how students are treated? Is there sarcasm? Is there humor, and are there smiles? Consider the answers to these and related questions and you get a fairly powerful sense of the degree to which the culture is conducive to learning, caring, and working hard—or not.

Then sit in on your department's monthly meeting. Is there a written, shared agenda? How much time is allocated to schedules and budgets and textbook orders and the latest dictates from the administration? How much time is allocated to discussions of "tricky and troublesome topics" or "an amazing app" that one colleague models for everyone else or a ten-minute video of a colleague's lesson the day before that is presented for analysis and critique? Obviously, some of these agenda items have nothing to do with the quality of teaching and learning or the development of a collaborative culture of improvement and mutual support among the members of the department. And just as obviously, other agenda items characterize a department as a team of professionals forever striving to build a culture of quality, mutual respect, and ongoing improvement.

The answers to these and other questions about classroom practice and department meetings provide a clear sense of the culture you establish and within which you work. They tell us about the norms and behaviors and expectations. They tell us whether there is a common shared culture or an "I'm okay, you're okay" laissez-faire approach. But regardless of the specific answers to such questions, it should be clear that culture dominates. To invigorate high school mathematics requires examining and adjusting culture.

Questions to Ask Yourselves

- How would you describe the dominant aspects of the culture within your classroom?

- How does your description align with or differ from descriptions provided by other members of the department?

- How would you describe the collective culture of your mathematics department?

- What suggestions do you have for enhancing this culture and creating a healthier and more productive environment?

Scope

GUIDING PRINCIPLE

The high school mathematics program must focus on the essential ideas and processes of mathematics. There must be an emphasis on the development of understanding and application of important content, rather than an effort to teach too much too quickly and with too little depth. Mathematics topics may be considered important for different reasons, such as their usefulness in building foundations for developing other mathematical ideas, their value for representing and solving problems, their role in linking mathematics to other disciplines, and their ability to deepen students' appreciation of mathematics as a discipline and a human endeavor.

If we are to truly invigorate high school mathematics, it is essential that we acknowledge that it is essentially impossible to complete an entire textbook in any given high school mathematics course unless we race through the text at an absurd pace with little depth and few opportunities for application and modeling. That's why effective teachers, and wisely developed curricula and pacing guides, use the textbook only as a resource and not a bible, identifying which chapters and which lessons must be skipped in order to make the course teachable. Similarly, it is essential that we acknowledge that most high school courses—particularly those outlined in the pernicious Appendix A of the Common Core—are, with almost sixty standards per course, essentially unteachable. We—effective teachers and knowledgeable curriculum developers—must use our experience to design truly teachable courses that employ technological tools, minimize obsolete skills, and focus on depth of understanding, problem solving, and modeling, leaving ample time for activities, tasks, projects, and discussions that support learning.

That is why, as we argued in Chapter 1 and suggest later in Chapters 4 and 5, our course proposals do not include such topics as factoring binomials with leading coefficients not equal to 1, division of polynomials and synthetic division, trigonometric identities, memorizing theorems (as opposed to selecting, using, and proving them), rationalizing denominators, and using pencil and paper to solve equations that technology can solve far more efficiently. We advocate for courses with a maximum of six units a year, with approximately thirty days per unit, so that there is adequate time to explore, teach, and learn mathematics in depth.

Questions to Ask Yourselves

- For which courses in your mathematics department do you feel there is an unreasonable amount of mathematics to "cover"? Why does this situation exist?

- Which of the topics that you currently teach have questionable value for students?

- Can you try to organize each existing high school mathematics course into five or six approximately thirty-day units? What must be eliminated in order to accomplish this?

Differentiation

GUIDING PRINCIPLE

The high school mathematics program must be built around a common core of essential and important mathematics differentiated by life and career goals. It must be delivered through a balance of shared experiences for all students and learning tasks that are appropriately chosen to reflect the prior knowledge of the students and respond to and build on that knowledge. Differentiation requires creating, modeling, adapting, and enriching instruction so that it engages the student, corrects misconceptions, sustains interest, and promotes confidence and perseverance.

We start with the simple reality that there are plus or minus twenty-five distinct brains in every class of students. We add the obvious truism that "one size never fits, doesn't fit, and can't ever fit all." And we conclude that we can only maximize the learning of mathematics by differentiating.

To people who have never taught or who choose to ignore the realities of socially mediated learning, differentiation is as simple as placing every student on a personalized computer with a personalized program. That is *not* how we perceive differentiation. Rather, recognizing both the differences among any class of students and the need for interaction and collaborative learning opportunities, we argue that differentiation is as simple and as challenging as a continuous focus on alternative approaches and multiple representations. Given that the one right way to get the one right answer has never served all students, effective teachers have always differentiated by asking "Who did it differently?" to elicit alternative approaches. And given that limiting instruction to only symbolic representations of mathematics has also never served all students, effective teachers have always differentiated by asking "How did you see that?" and "Who saw that differently?" to elicit a broader range of representations. We have touched upon this critical instructional shift in the discussion of vision earlier in this chapter, and we return to it in Chapter 6, on issues of pedagogy.

But differentiation is not just a classroom practice—it must also be built into a set of pathways that honor our students' different mathematical needs and future aspirations. We describe such a set of differentiated pathways in Chapter 5.

Questions to Ask Yourselves

- In what ways does our department's standard practice reflect a one-size-fits-all approach?
- In what ways does our department differentiate to maximize the opportunity for all students to learn?

Integrated Mathematics

GUIDING PRINCIPLE

The high school mathematics program must recognize that mathematics is a unified body of knowledge about quantity, change, uncertainty, shape, and dimension—or more formally, number, variables and functions, probability and data, and geometry and measurement. We have packaged this knowledge into algebra, geometry, and statistics silos, ignoring the connections between these silos and the power of making links between and among the different strands of the mathematical sciences.

One of the great mysteries of high school mathematics in the United States is how an integrated K–8 curriculum that balances number, algebra, data, shape, and measurement every year culminates in a high school program that ignores integration and resorts to Algebra 1, Geometry, Algebra 2, and Precalculus silos as the privileged pathway. No other industrialized, first-world country in the world follows this approach; instead, they use an integrated curriculum through grade 12. While the United States places AP Calculus on the pinnacle of achievement, much of the rest of the world, including many countries that far outperform the United States, considers the integrated International Baccalaureate (IB) program the gold standard for achievement.

Our strong bias toward an integrated program stems from

- the difficulty of inserting enough statistics and data analysis into the traditional program

- the reality that geometry would be well served with two-thirds of the time it now has

- the critical need to significantly increase the connections between and among the different domains of mathematics.

With more algebra taught in eighth grade than ever before and statistical literacy increasingly recognized as a critical component of mathematical understanding, an integrated approach makes even more sense. We suggest how this integration can be accomplished in Chapters 4 and 5, where we propose a common, integrated mathematics sequence of courses in grades 9 and 10, followed by differentiated pathways of courses in grades 11 and 12 that embrace appropriate connections between algebra, geometry, statistics, and topics in discrete mathematics.

Questions to Ask Yourselves

- Why do we cling to the traditional sequence as the core of high school mathematics for the vast majority of students?

- What are some of the distinct advantages *and* disadvantages of moving to an integrated approach, particularly in grades 9 and 10?

- What is the decision-making process in your school or district that could lead to a shift from the traditional sequence to an integrated approach?

Content and Process Standards

GUIDING PRINCIPLE

The high school mathematics program must be driven by standards or expectations that delineate the learning goals for each course and each unit within each course. Standards—both those that describe content and those that focus on process or practice—are the skeleton of a program and delineate specifically what students should know and be able to do as a result of completing a unit or course. These standards or learning goals guide decisions about how to use a textbook, what supplemental materials are necessary, and the content of all assessments.

We have come a very long way in moving from textbook-driven mathematics courses to standards-driven mathematics courses. Way back in 1989, NCTM's *Curriculum and Evaluation Standards for School Mathematics* began the national movement toward more precise descriptions of the expectations for student learning and introduced the radical notion of process standards to accompany content standards. It took two decades of meandering around in what proved to be valuable, but very general, grade-band statements of expectations to get to the Common Core State Standards for Mathematics in 2010 that, in terms of poker, "saw" NCTM and "raised" it with much greater specificity and guidance in the realms of both content and process/practice.

As we have noted, however, this specificity and guidance from the Common Core fell far short for grades 9–12, and many high school mathematics departments continue to wrestle with such critical questions as

- What specific content must be addressed in which course?

- What scope or number of standards is actually teachable, even with an hour a day?

- What progressions or trajectories of skills and concepts (a key feature of the K–8 standards) apply to 9–12?

- What balance should we strike between content and practice, and how are the critical practice standards interwoven into teaching the content?

Our curricula and our course guides must answer these questions. At their best they delineate content standards and describe, with examples, specifically what needs to be taught and learned, as well as the practices that transcend specific content and guide instruction.

When it comes to the more elusive process or practice standards, we are reminded of the progression from NCTM 1989 to NCTM 2000 to the Common Core in 2010, as shown in Figure 3.3. Moreover, even though most states have altered the original Common Core mathematics standards, every one of them has retained the mathematical practices as a key component of their state standards.

EVOLUTION OF PROCESS/PRACTICE STANDARDS

NCTM 1989 CURRICULUM AND EVALUATION STANDARDS	NCTM 2000 PRINCIPLES AND STANDARDS	2010 COMMON CORE STANDARDS FOR MATHEMATICAL PRACTICE
1. Problem solving 2. Reasoning 3. Communication 4. Connections	1. Problem solving 2. Reasoning 3. Communication 4. Connections 5. Representation	1. Make sense of problems and persevere in solving them. 2. Reason abstractly and quantitatively. 3. Construct viable arguments and critique the reasoning of others. 4. Model with mathematics. 5. Use appropriate tools strategically. 6. Attend to precision. 7. Look for and make use of structure. 8. Look for and express regularity in repeated reasoning.

FIGURE 3.3

We note, with respect to these practice/process standards, how much we all struggled to incorporate the original four 1989 process standards and how much confusion reigned on how and where to best address these critical elements of mathematics. We note that in 2000, NCTM recognized a giant hole and added representation, suggesting that these processes, like everything we do, need to be rethought and adapted over time. But once again, we struggled to address what were now five critical elements of mathematics. And then came the shift from "processes" to "practices" and the increase to *eight* practices proposed in the Common Core. If teachers were understandably overwhelmed with just four or five, how could anyone expect eight to take root in our classrooms?

Our advice is to limit expectations to what has a reasonable chance of being implemented, and to take seriously the risks of overwhelming professionals with too many expectations. Our advice is to make the first four Common Core Standards for Mathematical Practice the nonnegotiable overarching focus in everything we do in K–12 mathematics:

NONNEGOTIABLE

1. Make sense of problems and persevere in solving them.

2. Reason abstractly and quantitatively.

3. Construct viable arguments and critique the reasoning of others.

4. Model with mathematics.

Our purpose is *not* to belittle precision, tools, structure, and regularity, but to keep the focus on what matters most: problem solving, reasoning, argument, and modeling. Because there is so much that needs to be done to invigorate high school mathematics, when we can limit the demands, we increase the probability of effective implementation and success. Most importantly, we believe that these four statements capture exactly those practices that align with any set of updated goals or purposes for high school mathematics.

Just think about a society where every high school graduate could make sense of unfamiliar problems and persevere in solving them, reason abstractly and quantitatively, construct viable arguments and comfortably critique the reasoning of others, and use mathematical understanding to model real-world phenomena. What a world that would be, and what a wonderful goal to which every teacher of high school mathematics might aspire!

Questions to Ask Yourselves

- How successful have you and your colleagues been in implementing the vision of the eight Common Core Standards for Mathematical Practice?

- Have you and your colleagues had discussions and arguments about whether all eight practices are equally important? If not, why?

- If you start with our proposed four practices, how might you and your colleagues revise and adjust these practices for implementation in your department?

Connections

GUIDING PRINCIPLE

The high school mathematics program must include explicit and coherent exploration of how one piece of mathematics relates to other pieces of mathematics. It must effectively organize and integrate important mathematical ideas so that students grasp how the concepts, skills, and logical thinking build on and connect to each other.

A core, but often ignored, tenet of educational psychology is that we learn by connecting new knowledge to previously learned knowledge and that we develop new understandings by building on connections to existing understandings. Without connections, each bit of knowledge sits alone, making it much harder to process and more difficult to apply. Effective teachers have forever asked, "How is this like what we have already studied?" and "How is this similar to and different from this previous body of knowledge?" They are fostering connections and strengthening the mental power of learners of all ages.

Back in 1989, NCTM's *Curriculum and Evaluation Standards for School Mathematics* stated for Standard 4: Mathematical Connections in grades 9–12 that

> the mathematics curriculum should include investigations of the connections and interplay among various mathematical topics and their applications so that students can:
>
> - recognize equivalent representations of the same concept;
> - relate procedures in one representation to procedures in an equivalent representation;
> - use and value the connections among mathematical topics;
> - use and value the connections between mathematics and other disciplines. (146)

For the same standard eleven years later, in NCTM's updated *Principles and Standards for School Mathematics* (2000), we find:

> When students can see the connections across different mathematical content areas, they develop a view of mathematics as an integrated whole. As they build on their previous mathematical understandings while learning new concepts, students become increasingly aware of the connections among various mathematical topics. As students' knowledge of mathematics, their ability to use a wide range of mathematical representations, and their access to sophisticated technology and software increase, the connections they make with other academic disciplines, especially the sciences and social sciences, give them greater mathematical power. (354)

It is hard to imagine teaching the distributive property as only a symbolic rule that $a(b + c) = ab + ac$ without also showing and calculating the areas of a rectangle with length $b + c$ and width a that concretely models the area of the entire rectangle $(a(b + c))$ and the area of the two parts $(ab + ac)$. Similarly, teaching completing the square without pausing and completing a physical square with algebra tiles ignores the power of connections and borders on malpractice (see Figure 3.4).

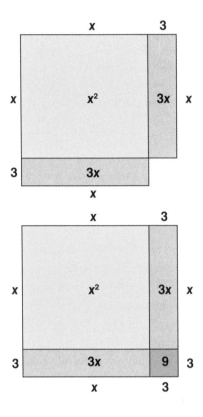

FIGURE 3.4

Questions to Ask Yourselves

- In a recent unit you taught, what opportunities did you use to make connections between mathematical topics, among equivalent representations, and between mathematics and other disciplines?

- In the next unit you will be teaching, what opportunities do you foresee for making connections between mathematical topics, among equivalent representations, and between mathematics and other disciplines?

Context and Modeling

GUIDING PRINCIPLE

The high school mathematics program must include situations, applications, and contemporary problems, often interdisciplinary in nature, that illustrate the usefulness of mathematics and employ mathematical modeling. Relevant contexts include worthwhile mathematical tasks, interesting applications, real-world opportunities to employ mathematical modeling, and problem-based lessons that motivate learning.

Traditional practice in high school mathematics is to spend days learning procedures by which to manipulate symbols before ever getting a glimpse at where and why these procedures have value. In the old days, it could have been argued that without facility with the procedures, there was no way to solve the problems and applications that used the procedures. In today's world, it is relating problem situations or applications to appropriate concepts that matters. It is mathematizing situations into equations or diagrams that matters. And it is the available technology, not procedural competence, that empowers students. For example, simply teaching statistical techniques in the abstract without tying these techniques to real-world situations and context, including, for example, predicting and analyzing election results, deprives our students of critical connections that strengthen both the depth of learning and the motivation to learn more.

Consider how much time is spent preparing students to solve the following exponential equation:

$$\text{Solve for } t\text{: } 16(.75)^t < 1$$

Now consider students working in pairs, wrestling with the following problem:

> **You ingest 16 mg of a controlled substance at 8 a.m. Your body metabolizes 25% of the substance every hour. Will you pass a 4 p.m. drug test that requires a level of less than 1 mg? At what time could you first pass the test?**

In lieu of taking the log of both sides and remembering a bunch of properties for simplification, in today's world all students can use a free online scientific calculator to see what happens to the value of $16(.75)^t$ as time increases from, say, 1 to 12 hours and arrive at a very reasonable approximation for *t*. Or students can just as easily use a free online graphing calculator to home in on the intersection of $y = 16(.75)^t$ and $y = 1$ (see Figure 3.5). With the calculations relegated to technology, the important work *that technology cannot replace* becomes solving realistic problems by creating a mathematical model for the situation, understanding that a rate of metabolism of 25% means that 75% of the substance remains, creating a model—the equation—that mathematizes that understanding, and using your model to solve the problem and potentially extend it to solving other problems.

Ask students why they often connect positively with high school statistics and they will tell you that it is the real data, realistic contexts, and practical problems that allow them to apply their statistical understanding. Then consider how rarely we find realistic contexts and practical problems in a year of precalculus, unless one considers utterly contrived "applications" that are usually little more than exercises disguised with words. We provide many more contextual and modeling examples in Part 3 when we address pedagogy, assessment, technology, and modeling.

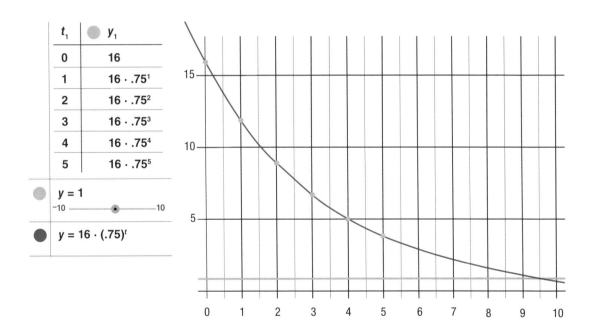

FIGURE 3.5

Questions to Ask Yourselves

- In recent lessons you have taught, how well have you balanced practical applications, mathematical modeling, and realistic contexts with the more typical skills of the lesson or unit?

- How often do you begin a lesson or a unit with a contextual example or application rather than focusing on skills first?

- Why, with all the access our students have to technological tools, do you think we still tend to emphasize skills over applications in our individual lessons, units, and assessments?

Assessment

GUIDING PRINCIPLE

The high school mathematics program must recognize assessment as an integral part of instruction. At its core, what we assess and how we assess it communicate most clearly what we value. Accordingly, assessments must include a balanced portfolio of strategically aligned, common, and high-quality summative unit assessments and an array of quizzes and benchmark tasks and other formative assessment techniques.

Another truism in life is that "what is inspected is respected." In schools, it is our assessments that tell students what we are inspecting and how we are inspecting it. These assessments clarify exactly what we deem important. And these assessments clarify what students need to respect by exerting the effort it takes to learn and master new content. How often do we hear, "Will this be on the test?" And good luck to any teacher who tries to maintain student interest after answering, "No, this is just enrichment."

But most importantly, we seek to debunk the idea of "first we teach, then we test, and finally we grade," as if these are three separate and distinct activities. Instead, we believe that instruction and assessment are not separate components of teaching, but integrally linked pieces of effective teaching and learning. That is, our decisions about what to teach and what to assess should go hand in hand. The alignment of our instructional goals, our instructional practices and tasks, and our assessments must be strong.

Effective teachers start the planning process by building clarity about the lesson goals and draft an exit ticket assessment that reflects the lesson goal *before* selecting tasks, examples, and exercises. Similarly, effective teachers *begin* unit planning with the unit assessment fully in mind and then adjust the unit assessment to reflect what they have learned from daily exit tickets.

We noted in the equity and access domain the practice of retesting. We look at this practice, as well as the critical role of common, high-quality unit assessments, in Chapter 7.

Questions to Ask Yourselves

- Is there a system of common, high-quality unit assessments for every course offered by your department? If not, why?

- Is it considered nonnegotiable that nearly every lesson concludes with an exit ticket or some other form of formative assessment to answer the simple question "What evidence do you have that this lesson was successful?" If not, why?

- Is there a system of retesting available to students for every unit assessment? Why or why not?

Technology

GUIDING PRINCIPLE

The high school mathematics program must make full use of technologies that increase the productivity of instruction and enrich students' experiences. The use of smartphones, calculators, computers, data-gathering tools and probes, interactive software, and real-time student data should be pervasive throughout instruction and assessment.

The availability of technology has changed the world. It has changed the workplace and both the availability of and expectations for jobs. It has opened new domains of study and supported incredible advances in medicine and science and commerce. It is technology—in conjunction with mathematics—that allows an Amazon order placed online at 10 a.m. to be delivered by 4 p.m. the same day or an Uber driver to arrive at your exact location in four minutes. It is technology, in the form of a single smartphone, that provides instantaneous, handheld access to an encyclopedia, a radio, a music collection, a mirror, a map, an atlas, a camera, magazines, a library of books, a calculator, a movie theater, a wireless phone, and so much more.

And yet there remains a wide range of practices and policies when it comes to technology in high school mathematics classrooms. We still fiercely debate whether students should be allowed access to their smartphones in mathematics classes, instead requiring them to lug around $129 graphing calculator bricks that have not decreased in price in nearly twenty years. We know that free interactive software such as Desmos activities is widely available, but it is not used everywhere. We know that high-stakes tests are increasingly delivered online and that available assessment technology can accurately score a range of constructed response items, but we cling to pencil-and-paper assessments that have scarcely changed in forty years.

We look at technology and the many ways it has become an indispensable component of effective teaching and learning of mathematics in Chapter 8.

Questions to Ask Yourselves

- What are your department policies on the use of technology to support teaching and learning in mathematics courses?

- What restrictions or limitations are in place for access to technology, and can they really be justified?

- How are video, online lessons, and free online supplemental resources used to support the teaching and learning of mathematics in every course in your department?

Adequate Time

GUIDING PRINCIPLE

The high school mathematics program must have adequate time to effectively meet the learning standards and implement the vision of teaching and learning that guides our work. It is not possible to accomplish what high school mathematics is expected to accomplish with anything less than 60 minutes of allocated time each day or the equivalent of 160 hours of classroom contact time for each course.

There is so much we know about how much time is needed, how much is typically available, and how it is typically spent. Most discussions about time start and end with "We don't control the length of a classroom period, so we have to live with what we are given." Our argument is that, from the perspective of both students' and society's needs, mathematics—when done right—is second in importance only to English/language arts. Treating mathematics, as is so often the case, as just another 46-minute period in a crowded day fails to recognize the scope of essential content and the critical need for interactive and collaborative practices that develop understanding, maintain interest, and support deeper learning.

When we conduct demonstration classes in which we are presented with a 45-minute class period, we start out stressed, and no matter how narrow our learning goal, we start looking at the clock. We eliminate opening activities, or we skimp on a discussion of the learning goal, or we cut short the time students need to solve and process, or we fall behind the clock and skip the all-important formative assessment. We cheat our students when we use time as the excuse for racing through the curriculum by showing, telling, and assigning practice.

When we have 60 minutes, we find ourselves much more likely to accomplish our goals. We have time to launch the lesson with a number talk or a cumulative review. We spend 2 minutes being clear about the day's learning goal and create an anticipatory set for the lesson. We even find time to joke or check in with students to support a safe environment that is conducive to learning. We then have time for two solid 20-minute lesson chunks before asking students to "turn and tell your partner what you learned today" and, finally, to complete a formative assessment exit ticket. Try doing all that in 45 minutes and no wonder teachers burn out!

We note the need for 160 hours for each course on the assumption that assemblies, field trips, mandated testing, delayed openings, and other assorted interruptions steal something close to 20 days in each course. Then, assuming that something close to 10 percent of instructional time is devoted to tests and quizzes, we end up with about 140 hours of non-assessment instructional time as the standard for which to strive.

When teachers have 45 minutes per day or 90-minute blocks every other day for 160 actual days without interruption, we are talking about 75 percent of the time that students with 60-minute periods are provided. There is no getting around the inequity among schools and districts, and thus for students, when the difference between 45 minutes and 60 minutes each day is so huge.

But of course, any discussion of time must also address how the time is spent. We urge teachers to launch 60-minute lessons with warm-up activities like number talks and cumulative review. We strongly urge all high school teachers to draw from released SAT and ACT examinations for warm-up tasks. We hope that going over homework is never a time-wasting 15- to 20-minute ordeal, but instead entails teachers posting the answers to the homework exercises or problems on the whiteboard and providing students with 5 minutes to review their work in pairs or triads, with particular attention to the most troublesome problems. Correct work for any problems that are still causing trouble can be easily displayed with a document camera and discussed before homework is collected, only to be recorded as completed. When two or three 15- or 20-minute instructional chunks draw from such options as lecture, games, video, online activities, selective practice, or project work, teachers acknowledge the limited attention span of adolescents and mix things up to maintain interest and to differentiate among approaches.

Questions to Ask Yourselves

- How many minutes are allocated to mathematics each day or every two days?

- How does this allocation compare to an average of 60 minutes per day?

- What discussions need to be conducted and what arguments need to be made to narrow the gap between current time allocations and 60 minutes per day?

- How do teachers use the time they have, and what consistency is there among members of the department on how time is allocated to specific elements of a typical lesson?

Professional Growth and Collaboration

GUIDING PRINCIPLE

The high school mathematics program must be supported by intensive attention to ongoing professional growth and collaboration among the mathematics teachers. In today's world, particularly in light of the technological opportunities and new differentiated courses being proposed, it is impossible to believe that any one teacher of mathematics can do it all. Accordingly, within every high school mathematics department there must be structures and practices including course committees, allocated time for collaborative planning, video and video reviews, and an expectation of collegial classroom visits and follow-up debrief discussions.

As teachers, our professional isolation within a dominant culture of "I'm okay, you're okay, don't bother me and I won't bother you" is the single greatest obstacle to change and improvement. Given the challenges of making mathematics work for *all* students, and the changes necessary to enact this goal, it is no longer acceptable to allow professional isolation to exist; nor can we continue the practice of treating our classrooms as personal castles surrounded by shark-infested moats. Instead, the dominant mantra must be "We're all in this together and what any one of us does affects what the rest of us can and cannot do."

Ask yourself, how often have you sat in a colleague's classroom for an entire lesson? When have you placed an iPad on a tripod or Swivl in the back of your room and just let it record a lesson that you later reviewed in the quiet of your personal space or that you shared with colleagues? Could you and a colleague interdependently plan and revise each unit? These are practices that we see in highly effective high schools. These are the practices that we return to in Chapter 10, where we focus on an implementation game plan.

The message we seek to convey is that changes of the magnitude we advocate take time and collaboration. Just as our goal statements pay homage to the "development of lifelong learners," as teachers we must commit ourselves to the same lifelong learning to stay current and vital in a changing world.

Accordingly, we end this section of guiding principles or domains of invigoration with one of our favorite quotes from NCTM's *Principles to Actions* (2014):

> In an excellent mathematics program, educators hold themselves and their colleagues accountable for the mathematical success of every student and for personal and collective professional growth toward effective teaching and learning of mathematics. A professional does not accept the status quo, even when it is reasonably good, and continually seeks to learn and grow. (99)

Questions to Ask Yourselves

- What collaborative structures are in place within your department to support a culture of sharing and professional interaction?
- What collaborative structures, such as course committees, video reviews, collegial classroom visits, and dedicated planning time, are not currently in place? Why do you think this is, and what can you do to change this?
- Do you observe colleagues on a regular basis and conduct a debrief session following each observation?

Conclusion

We would be completely irresponsible to suggest that all fourteen of these changes should, or even can, be tackled at once. Every high school we know has made progress on some of these changes and has miles to go on others. Change of this magnitude cannot be mandated "by the end of the year" or even "within the next two years." What we *do* know is that some of these changes enable other ones. For example, without addressing adequate time, acting on "less is more," or focusing more on the first four practice standards, real progress is unlikely. Similarly, without attending to building a shared sense of goals and purpose as well as a written vision, shifts in courses, content, instruction, and assessment are unlikely to be coordinated and effective. And without significant shifts in the departmental culture around professional growth and collaboration, teachers end up being told what to do without the requisite understanding, support, and buy-in.

The remainder of this book describes in greater detail what many of these proposed changes look like in classrooms, departments, and schools. Our goal is to provide guidance and examples for making these changes, for stimulating professional discussions, and for supporting the gradual implementation and institutionalization of each of these needed changes.

Guiding Questions

1. Of these fourteen domains, which ones do you think your department comes closest to meeting? In what ways is this the case?

2. Of these fourteen domains, which ones do you think your department is farthest from meeting? Why do you think this is the case? What specific steps can you take to change this?

3. Of these fourteen domains, and given that it is impossible to simultaneously address them all, which two or three do you and your colleagues believe are good places to start?

It is clear that the status quo is
no longer acceptable and major
changes in course organization,
mathematical content, pedagogy,
and assessment are long overdue.

—STEVEN LEINWAND AND ERIC MILOU

Part 2

Content, Courses, and Pathways

Anybody who has read up to this point should be screaming, "Okay! Enough already! I agree with a lot of what you have described and I recognize that there is a lot that needs to be changed. But what exactly do you expect me to actually be teaching? That is, given all the challenges that have been outlined and the guiding principles proposed, what exactly do common, integrated mathematics courses for grades 9 and 10 look like, and what specifically is included in those courses that constitute differentiated, rigorous pathways for grades 11 and 12?"

In Chapters 4 and 5, these are exactly the questions we attempt to answer with far more specificity and justification than are found in either the high school section of the Common Core State Standards, NCTM's *Catalyzing Change in High School Mathematics* (2018), or typical state mathematics curriculum frameworks. Enough work on these challenges has been done to allow us to draw from a range of resources, programs, and projects to attempt credible, comprehensive, and teachable options that are all designed to stimulate the invigoration of high school mathematics.

4

Ninety percent of the data we have in the world right now was created in the past two years. We're at a point where things are changing and we need to help students navigate that new world.

—JO BOALER (2019)

Grades 9 and 10

A Common Curriculum for All

Where We Are Starting From

When we turn to the all-important first two years of high school, we draw on three key ideas.

First, we take domains 1, 3, 5, 7, 8, 9, 10, and 12 from Chapter 3 to heart. That is, suppose we think in terms of broader goals, more access and equity, a reasonable and teachable scope (focusing on key content progressions from K–8 to grades 11 and 12), an integrated approach, clear standards, a focus on connections, attention to context, and incorporation of technology. What would all that mean for the first two years of high school?

Second, we make some key assumptions about traditional Algebra 1 and Geometry and current needs:

- As equations and functions are increasingly taught in middle school, there is ample room for adjusting what has traditionally been Algebra 1.

- For years, many teachers of geometry have questioned the need for an entire year focusing on geometry, particularly the time devoted to formal two-column proofs and to revisiting surface area and volume.

- Statistics needs much more emphasis.

- Technology allows for less time spent on rote skills and procedures and a much greater emphasis on applications and modeling.

- As the need for mathematics grows due to the demands of citizenship and the workplace, there is content (linear functions, similarity, exponential growth, and standard deviation, to name only a few) that *all* students should be expected to understand and apply.

Third, our plan must account for and support *both* acceleration and enrichment for some students *and* double-period boost-up opportunities for others who arrive with serious gaps.

Based on these ideas and the concerns we've discussed in previous chapters, we now turn to detailed descriptions of what Integrated High School Mathematics 1 and Integrated High School Mathematics 2 might look like.

No One Answer or Silver Bullet

Our specific proposals for the two courses for grades 9 and 10 must be seen as discussion fodder for course creation and *not* manna from heaven or the perfect answers. However, we are convinced that it is much, much more difficult to start with a blank page than it is to have a credible, worked-out example as the starting point, and so we aim to provide you with such an example.

We do not claim that these are the only big ideas or the exact right set of essential understandings. We do not claim that our proposals for instructional units are the only way to organize two years of content. And we understand that depending upon the number of minutes allocated to mathematics, it may be necessary to delete some of our proposals or perhaps even add topics or understandings without undermining the scope principle discussed in Chapter 3.

We do claim, however, that the specifics outlined in this chapter represent a significant improvement over the status quo. Additionally, we claim that these ideas do not emerge from thin air and pipe dreams, but are drawn from work we have seen or supported in schools, states, and countries around the world. And we claim that adopting most, if not all, of these recommendations can make a significant difference in students' lives, dispositions toward mathematics, and measures of achievement.

Big Ideas and Essential Understandings

We can't imagine designing coherent grades 9 and 10 mathematics experiences that don't progress coherently from, and aren't vertically articulated with, grade 8 mathematics experiences. While it is common practice to begin curriculum development with chapters or units, we argue that delineating big ideas and essential understandings is a necessary first step in creating coherent trajectories, before moving on to clustering these big ideas and essential understandings into units. We also argue that common grades 9 and 10 courses that honor our guiding principles must ensure a balance of skills, concepts, and applications at every point—a goal met by examining big ideas and essential understandings instead of a list of skills.

Using the same approach that we have employed with numerous high school mathematics departments over the past decade, we begin by reviewing and drawing from the 9–12 Common Core State Standards and from *Catalyzing Change in High School Mathematics* (NCTM 2018). We then turn to the increasing wealth of online resources such as Contemporary Mathematics in Context (Core-Plus), Illustrative Math, the Mathematics Visions Project, and Geoff Krall's Emergent Math Integrated Courses. And we check our work against the emerging and innovative high school curriculum guidance found in Oregon, Oklahoma, Ohio, and Alabama that propose new courses and pathways. Distilling this broad array of input, we summarize the big ideas and essential understandings, breaking them down by algebraic, geometric, and statistical domains (see Figure 4.1) as a starting place and with the understanding that (1) we need to use this data to create coherent progressions from grade 8 to grade 10, and (2) this data will then need to be intentionally whittled down and shaped into coherent units of instruction and reasonable amounts of content to create two common, teachable mathematics courses.

BIG IDEAS AND ESSENTIAL UNDERSTANDINGS IN GRADE 8 AND GRADES 9 AND 10
(THE ESSENTIAL CORE MATHEMATICAL CONTENT THAT ALL STUDENTS NEED TO PROCEED)

DOMAIN	GRADE 8	GRADES 9 AND 10
Numerical Ideas and Understandings	Big Ideas: • There is an inverse relationship between exponents and roots. • All rational and irrational numbers can be ordered and approximately placed on a number line. • A set of properties about integer exponents can be derived and applied. • Many real-world situations and phenomena can be modeled mathematically.	

FIGURE 4.1

BIG IDEAS AND ESSENTIAL UNDERSTANDINGS IN GRADE 8 AND GRADES 9 AND 10, *cont.*

DOMAIN	GRADE 8	GRADES 9 AND 10
Numerical Ideas and Understandings	Essential Understandings: ▪ Together rational and irrational numbers complete the real number system, representing all points on the number line. ▪ Just as multiplying means repetitive addition, using an exponent means repetitive multiplication. ▪ Mathematical modeling and quantitative reasoning require attention to constants, variables, and units of measure.	
Algebraic Ideas and Understandings	Big Ideas: ▪ A function is a powerful tool that can relate an input to exactly one output. ▪ Linear functions can be expressed in words, equations, tables, and graphs. ▪ Systems of linear equations have either no solutions, a single solution, or an infinite number of solutions. ▪ The equation of a line can be generated from any two points on that line. ▪ When the variable moves from being a linear coefficient to being an exponent, linear functions become exponential functions and lines become curves.	Big Ideas: ▪ Functions can be described by using a variety of representations: mapping diagrams, function notation (e.g., $f(x) = x^2$), recursive definitions, tables, and graphs. ▪ The structure of an equation or inequality (including, but not limited to, one-variable linear and quadratic equations, inequalities, and systems of linear equations in two variables) can be purposefully analyzed (with and without technology) to determine an efficient strategy to find a solution, if one exists, and then to justify the solution. ▪ Functions model a wide variety of real situations and can help students understand the processes of making and changing assumptions, assigning variables, and finding solutions to contextual problems. ▪ Linear relationships, including arithmetic sequences, represent additive change and have a constant slope or rate of change; in contrast, exponential relationships, including geometric sequences, represent multiplicative change and have increasing or decreasing slopes or rates of change.

FIGURE 4.1, *continued*

continues

BIG IDEAS AND ESSENTIAL UNDERSTANDINGS IN GRADE 8 AND GRADES 9 AND 10, *cont.*

DOMAIN	GRADE 8	GRADES 9 AND 10
Algebraic Ideas and Understandings	Essential Understandings: ■ Properties of numbers are used to create equivalent expressions and find solutions of linear equations. ■ Proportional relationships, lines that contain (0,0), and functions in the form of $y = mx$ are equivalent representations. ■ The features of linear functions can be identified in verbal, symbolic, graphical, and tabular representations (e.g., where does the 2 in $P = 2T + 5$ appear in verbal, tabular, and graphical forms of this function?). ■ The meaning of slope and intercept of linear functions can be interpreted in terms of the context of the linear function.	Essential Understandings: ■ Expressions can be rewritten in equivalent forms and equations can be solved by using algebraic properties, including properties of addition, multiplication, and exponentiation, to make different characteristics or features visible. ■ Finding solutions to an equation, inequality, or system of equations or inequalities requires the checking of candidate solutions, whether generated analytically or graphically, to ensure that solutions are found and that those found are not extraneous. ■ Expressions, equations, and inequalities can be used to analyze and make predictions, both within mathematics and as mathematics is applied in different contexts—in particular, contexts that arise in relation to linear, quadratic, and exponential situations. ■ Functions shift the emphasis from considering a point-by-point relationship between two variables (input/output) to considering an entire set of ordered pairs (where each first element is paired with exactly one second element) as an entity with its own features and characteristics. ■ When graphed, every linear relationship can be expressed as a translation (slide) and a rotation of the $y = x$ line or parent function and every quadratic relationship can be expressed as a set of transformations of the $y = x^2$ parabola or parent function. ■ Different, but equivalent, forms of linear functions, including $y = mx + b$, $ax + by = c$, and $(y - y_1) = a(x - x_1)$, and quadratic functions, including $y = ax^2 + bx + c$, $y = a(x - h)^2 + k$, and $y = a(x - r)(x - s)$, reveal different aspects of the function.

FIGURE 4.1, *continued*

BIG IDEAS AND ESSENTIAL UNDERSTANDINGS IN GRADE 8 AND GRADES 9 AND 10, *cont.*

DOMAIN	GRADE 8	GRADES 9 AND 10
Algebraic Ideas and Understandings		Essential Understandings, *continued*: • Graphs can be used to obtain exact or approximate solutions of equations, inequalities, and systems of equations and inequalities—including systems of linear equations in two variables and systems of linear and quadratic equations (given or obtained by using technology). • Functions that are members of the same family have distinguishing attributes (structures) common to all functions within that family. • Functions can be represented graphically, and key features of the graphs, including zeros, intercepts, and, when relevant, rate of change and maximum/minimum values, can be associated with and interpreted in terms of the equivalent symbolic representation.
Geometric Ideas and Understandings	Big Ideas: • Reflections, translations, rotations, dilations, and combinations of these transformations are actions that have properties. • There are many ways to prove the Pythagorean theorem. • All three-dimensional figures have surface area and volume that can be calculated with appropriate measures and formulas.	Big Ideas: • Areas and volumes of figures can be computed by determining how the figure might be obtained from simpler figures by dissection and recombining. • Applying geometric transformations to figures provides opportunities for describing the attributes of the figures preserved by the transformation and for describing symmetries by examining when a figure can be mapped onto itself. • Transformations in geometry serve as a connection with algebra, both through the concept of functions and through the analysis of graphs of functions as geometric figures. • Proof is the means by which we demonstrate whether a statement is true or false mathematically, and proofs can be communicated in a variety of ways (e.g., in two columns or in paragraphs). • Recognizing congruence, similarity, symmetry, measurement opportunities, and other geometric ideas, including right triangle trigonometry in real-world contexts, provides a means of building understanding of these concepts and is a powerful tool for solving problems related to the physical world in which we live.

FIGURE 4.1, *continued*

continues

BIG IDEAS AND ESSENTIAL UNDERSTANDINGS IN GRADE 8 AND GRADES 9 AND 10, *cont.*

DOMAIN	GRADE 8	GRADES 9 AND 10
Geometric Ideas and Understandings	Essential Understandings: • Congruence is based on rigid transformations of figures. • Similarity is based on dilations of figures. • Given the lengths of any two sides of a right triangle, the Pythagorean theorem can be used to find the length of the third side. • Lengths, widths, heights, and circumferences are one-dimensional measures; areas and surface areas are two-dimensional measures; and volume is a three-dimensional measure. • The formulas for surface area and volume can all be derived and modeled.	Essential Understandings: • Constructing approximations of measurements with different tools, including technology, can support an understanding of measurement. • When an object is the image of a known object under a similarity transformation, a length, area, or volume on the image can be computed by using proportional relationships. • Showing that two figures are congruent involves showing that there is a rigid motion (translation, rotation, reflection, or glide reflection) or, equivalently, a sequence of rigid motions that maps one figure to the other. • Showing that two figures are similar involves finding a similarity transformation (dilation or composite of a dilation with a rigid motion) or, equivalently, a sequence of similarity transformations that maps one figure onto the other. • Using technology to construct and explore figures with constraints provides an opportunity to explore the independence and dependence of assumptions and conjectures. • Proofs of theorems can sometimes be made with transformations, coordinates, or algebra; all approaches can be useful, and in some cases one may provide a more accessible or understandable argument than another. • Experiencing the mathematical modeling cycle in problems involving geometric concepts, from the simplification of the real problem to the solving of the simplified problem, the interpretation of its solution, and the checking of the solution's feasibility, introduces geometric techniques, tools, and points of view that are valuable in problem solving.

FIGURE 4.1, *continued*

BIG IDEAS AND ESSENTIAL UNDERSTANDINGS IN GRADE 8 AND GRADES 9 AND 10, *cont.*

DOMAIN	GRADE 8	GRADES 9 AND 10
Statistical Ideas and Understandings	Big Ideas: • A line is a first approximation for studying bivariate data. • Bivariate data can be graphed and approximated by equations that enable their interpretation and use for prediction. • Scatterplots of bivariate data can identify clustering, outliers, positive and negative association, and linear or nonlinear association.	Big Ideas: • Making and defending informed data-based decisions is a characteristic of a quantitatively literate person. • Data arise from a context and come in two types: quantitative (continuous or discrete) and categorical. Technology can be used to "clean" and organize data, including very large data sets, into a useful and manageable structure—a first step in any analysis of data. • Data-analysis techniques can be used to develop models of contextual situations and to generate and evaluate possible solutions to real problems involving those contexts. • Study designs are of three main types: sample survey, experiment, and observational study. • Scatterplots, including plots over time, can reveal patterns, trends, clusters, and gaps that are useful in analyzing the association between two contextual variables. • The role of randomization is different in randomly selecting samples and in randomly assigning subjects to experimental treatment groups. • The scope and validity of statistical inferences are dependent on the role of randomization in the study design. • Conditional probabilities—that is, those probabilities that are "conditioned" by some known information—can be computed from data organized in contingency tables. Conditions or assumptions may affect the computation of a probability.

FIGURE 4.1, *continued*

continues

BIG IDEAS AND ESSENTIAL UNDERSTANDINGS IN GRADE 8 AND GRADES 9 AND 10, *cont.*

DOMAIN	GRADE 8	GRADES 9 AND 10
Statistical Ideas and Understandings	Essential Understanding: • The degree to which a set of points approaches a straight line is called correlation.	Essential Understandings: • Mathematical and statistical reasoning about data can be used to evaluate conclusions and assess risks. • Distributions of quantitative data (continuous or discrete) in one variable should be described in the context of the data with respect to what is typical (the shape, with appropriate measures of center and variability, including standard deviation) and what is not (outliers), and these characteristics can be used to compare two or more subgroups with respect to a variable. • The association between two categorical variables is typically represented by using two-way tables and segmented bar graphs. • Analyzing the association between two quantitative variables should involve statistical procedures, such as examining (with technology) the sum of squared deviations in fitting a linear model, analyzing residuals for patterns, generating a least-squares regression line and finding a correlation coefficient, and differentiating between correlation and causation. • Bias, in sampling, responses, or nonresponses, may occur in surveys, yielding results that are not representative of the population of interest. • The larger the sample size, the smaller the expected variability in the sampling distribution of a sample statistic. • The sampling distribution of a sample statistic formed from repeated samples for a given sample size drawn from a population can be used to identify typical behavior for that statistic. Examining several such sampling distributions leads to estimating a set of plausible values for the population parameter, using the margin of error as a measure that describes the sampling variability.

FIGURE 4.1, *continued*

BIG IDEAS AND ESSENTIAL UNDERSTANDINGS IN GRADE 8 AND GRADES 9 AND 10, *cont.*

DOMAIN	GRADE 8	GRADES 9 AND 10
Statistical Ideas and Understandings		Essential Understandings, *continued*: ■ Simulation of sampling distributions by hand or with technology can be used to determine whether a statistic (or statistical difference) is significant in a statistical sense or whether it is surprising or unlikely to happen under the assumption that outcomes are occurring by random chance. ■ Two events are independent if the occurrence of one event does not affect the probability of the other event. Determining whether two events are independent is useful for finding and understanding probabilities.

FIGURE 4.1, *continued*

What is worth noticing in Figure 4.1:

■ The big ideas and essential understandings are overarching takeaways from one or two years of study. They are *not* intended to be skills or topics that can be taught in a day or a week of instruction. Rather, they emerge from tasks, discussions, and consolidation of learning and, when successful, last a lifetime, because they are deeply understood and not merely memorized.

■ We start with these ideas and understandings, drawing mostly from NCTM's *Catalyzing Change in High School Mathematics* (2018), because they are most often lost in the sea of skills and exercises that have undermined a depth of mathematical understanding. We will look at specific skills and concepts later in the chapter.

■ For grades 9 and 10, we identify seventeen big ideas and twenty-five essential understandings, a scope that we believe is a manageable and teachable set of expectations for two years of high school mathematics.

■ There is a distinct balance among the algebraic, the geometric, and the statistical that creates a strong and sturdy three-legged platform upon which to learn more specialized and less integrated mathematics in grades 11 and 12.

■ We have attempted to show clear progressions as students move from grade 8 to the first two years of high school.

- Finally, starting with a delineation of big ideas and essential understandings reinforces two critical ideas for invigorating high school math: first, our assessments must include tasks that focus, in part, on these ideas and understandings, and second, typical, traditional high school mathematics continues to emphasize far more procedural knowledge and symbol manipulation than is needed to thrive in today's world.

Core Units of Instruction

Big ideas and essential understandings do not live in isolation. Rather, they cluster into topical units of instruction that form the spine of every effective mathematics course. The typical chapter-by-chapter approach to high school mathematics offers little more than a lesson-by-lesson sequence of skills with a few applications sprinkled in and minimal attention to conceptual understanding. We, however, conceptualize large instructional units as boxes or containers for the tasks, problems, experiments, and projects that support the development of skills and competencies in the service of developing a much deeper level of mathematical literacy that encompasses the big ideas and essential understandings shown in Figure 4.1.

Figure 4.2 proposes a set of such instructional units, aligned with the scope domain discussed in Chapter 3, that provides clear, coherent trajectories of essential mathematics for all students from grade 8 to grade 10.

Things to note in Figure 4.2:

- It is clear that big ideas like place value or division in elementary school or proportional reasoning and equations in middle school cannot be adequately developed in one chapter or one unit in one year. That is why all effective standards develop these big ideas over two or even three years. The same holds true for the critical ideas of linear, exponential, and quadratic functions. The unit organization we propose introduces linear and exponential functions in grade 8 and then fully develops them in grade 9 (linear) and 10 (exponential). Similarly, we propose introducing quadratic functions in grade 9 and fully developing them in grade 10.

- In the spirit of the integration guiding principle, we propose a balance among algebraic, geometric, and statistical units in each grade.

- A key aspect of these courses, other than the balance among algebra, geometry, and statistics, is honoring the principle that "less is more" and that slowing down the rush through content is essential to shift the focus to deeper understanding,

PROPOSED UNITS OF INSTRUCTION IN GRADES 8, 9, AND 10
(HOW WE MIGHT CHUNK ESSENTIAL UNDERSTANDINGS INTO COHERENT UNITS)

GRADE 8	GRADE 9: INTEGRATED MATHEMATICS 1: THE STUDY OF PATTERNS	GRADE 10: INTEGRATED MATHEMATICS 2: FROM PATTERNS TO STRUCTURE
<ul><li>Linear Functions</li><li>Geometric Objects, Congruence, and Transformations</li><li>Real Numbers, Exponents, Roots, and Pythagoras</li><li>Linear Equations and Systems of Linear Equations</li><li>Volume and Surface Area</li><li>Introduction to Exponential Functions</li><li>Data Representations and Interpretation, Including Bivariate Data and Trend Lines</li></ul>	**Patterns in Data:** Single-variable data plots and calculating measures of center and variability	**Quadratic Functions and Models:** Quadratic equations and quadratic functions, maxima and minima, systems of linear and quadratic equations
	Patterns of Change: Bivariate data, using tables, graphs, and algebra to analyze patterns in variables that change over time, including linear functions and an introduction to nonlinear functions such as exponential and quadratic functions	**Patterns in Space:** Similarity, Pythagorean theorem, surface area and volume of three-dimensional polyhedrons, dilations, right triangle trigonometry
	Patterns in Shape: The language and tools of geometry, transformations, congruence, symmetry, circles, coordinate geometry, and constructions	**Exponential Functions and Models:** Geometric sequences; multiplicative change; comparing linear, quadratic, and exponential change; systems of linear and exponential equations
	Patterns in Chance: Probability and simulations	**Proofs, Inferences, and Data:** Inductive and deductive reasoning and statistical inferences
	Capstone: Inequalities and linear programming (fit lines and function rules to data)	**Capstone:** Using regression and correlation to analyze real data and build authentic models

FIGURE 4.2

application, modeling, and justification. That is why each of the two courses proposed in this chapter is limited to five units, each expected to take from six to seven weeks, giving teachers *and* students, with one hour of mathematics each day and the significant incorporation of technology, the needed time to move far beyond memorization and symbol manipulation.

- To address the big idea that "linear relationships, including arithmetic sequences, represent additive change and have a constant slope or rate of change; in contrast, exponential relationships, including geometric sequences, represent multiplicative change and have increasing or decreasing slopes or rates of change," we urge schools and districts to introduce linear and exponential functions in grade 8 to ensure students understand that there is much more to life than just linear functions.

- One of the banes of every high school mathematics teacher's existence is the "When are we ever going to use this?" question. Too often, students never really see meaningful applications. That is why in grade 9 we strongly advocate for a final unit on linear inequalities and linear programming. This is the perfect capstone to Integrated High School Mathematics 1 because it extends linear equations to linear inequalities, focuses on graphing more than on solving equations, and addresses modeling (identification of variables, constraints, and potential maximums or minimums), to provide a powerful platform for realistic problem solving that leaves most students actually believing that the mathematics they have learned in grade 9 has real applicability and value. Similarly, the capstone in Integrated High School Mathematics 2 uses regression and correlation to analyze real data and build authentic models.

Proposed Course Outline for Integrated High School Mathematics 1

Based on the big ideas, essential understandings, and proposed units in Figures 4.1 and 4.2, we propose the course outline for Integrated High School Mathematics 1 in Figure 4.3.

A PROPOSED COURSE OUTLINE FOR INTEGRATED HIGH SCHOOL MATHEMATICS 1

UNIT	TOPICS	ESSENTIAL CONTENT
UNIT 1: **Patterns in Data**	■ Single-variable data ■ Representing and describing data presented in bar graphs, histograms, and box plots ■ Measures of center and variability	■ Understand that data arise from a context and come in two types: quantitative (continuous or discrete) and categorical. ■ Represent data with plots on the real number line (dot plots, histograms, and box plots). ■ Use statistics appropriate to the shape of the data distribution to compare center (median, mean) and spread (interquartile range, standard deviation) of two or more different data sets. ■ Interpret differences in shape, center, and spread in the context of the data sets, accounting for possible effects of extreme data points (outliers).
UNIT 2: **Patterns of Change**	■ Bivariate data and using tables, graphs, and algebra to analyze patterns in variables that change over time ■ Scatterplots ■ Linear functions ■ Fitting lines and finding their equations ■ Representing linear, quadratic, and exponential functions in tables, graphs, and symbols, including analyzing first and second differences	■ Represent data on two quantitative variables on a scatterplot, and describe how the variables are related. ■ Fit a function to the data; use functions fitted to data to solve problems in the context of the data. Emphasize linear, quadratic, and exponential models. ■ Interpret the slope (rate of change) and the intercept (constant term) of a linear model in the context of the data. ■ Understand that the graph of an equation in two variables is the set of all its solutions plotted in the coordinate plane, often forming a curve (which could be a line). ■ Write a function that describes a relationship between two quantities. ■ Identify the effect on the graph of replacing $f(x)$ with $f(x) + k$, $k\,f(x)$, $f(kx)$, and $f(x + k)$ for specific values of k (both positive and negative); find the value of k given the graphs. ■ Distinguish between situations that can be modeled with linear functions and with nonlinear functions. ■ Understand that linear functions grow by equal differences over equal intervals, and examine how nonlinear functions grow.

FIGURE 4.3   *continues*

A PROPOSED COURSE OUTLINE FOR INTEGRATED HIGH SCHOOL MATHEMATICS 1, *cont.*

UNIT	TOPICS	ESSENTIAL CONTENT
UNIT 3: **Patterns in Shape**	<ul><li>The language and tools of geometry</li><li>Points, lines, planes, and space: from zero dimensions to three dimensions</li><li>Slope, distance, and midpoints</li><li>Classification of triangles and quadrilaterals</li><li>Transformations and congruence</li><li>Symmetry</li><li>Measuring circles</li><li>Coordinate geometry</li><li>Constructions</li></ul>	<ul><li>Know precise definitions of *angle, circle, perpendicular line, parallel line,* and *line segment.*</li><li>Prove basic theorems about lines and angles.</li><li>Understand midpoint, the distance formula, and properties/classifications of triangles and quadrilaterals.</li><li>Represent transformations in the plane.</li><li>Understand that showing that two figures are congruent involves demonstrating that there is a rigid motion (translation, rotation, reflection, or glide reflection) or, equivalently, a sequence of rigid motions that maps one figure to the other.</li><li>Apply geometric transformations to figures with the goals of describing the attributes of the figures preserved by the transformation and describing symmetries by examining when a figure can be mapped onto itself.</li><li>Identify and describe relationships among inscribed angles, radii, and chords.</li><li>Use the coordinate plane to visualize relationships between quantities and to build understandings of connections between algebraic statements and the functions or relationships that they express.</li><li>Make geometric constructions with a variety of tools and methods.</li></ul>
UNIT 4: **Patterns in Chance**	<ul><li>Calculating probability</li><li>Geometric probability</li><li>Relative frequencies</li><li>Conditional probability</li><li>Using simulations to calculate probability</li></ul>	<ul><li>Describe events as subsets of a sample space (the set of outcomes) using characteristics (or categories) of the outcomes, or as unions, intersections, or complements of other events ("or," "and," "not").</li><li>Understand that two events are independent if the occurrence of one event does not affect the probability of the other event. Determining whether two events are independent is useful for finding and understanding probabilities.</li><li>Compute conditional probabilities—that is, those probabilities that are "conditioned" by some known information—from data organized in contingency tables. Know that conditions or assumptions may affect the computation of a probability.</li></ul>

FIGURE 4.3, *continued*

A PROPOSED COURSE OUTLINE FOR INTEGRATED HIGH SCHOOL MATHEMATICS 1, *cont.*

UNIT	TOPICS	ESSENTIAL CONTENT
UNIT 5: **Capstone: Inequalities and Linear Programming**	■ Solving and graphing linear inequalities ■ Identifying variables, constants, and constraints in mathematical situations ■ Setting up and solving linear programming problems	■ Understand that the structure of an equation or inequality (including, but not limited to, one-variable linear and quadratic equations, inequalities, and systems of linear equations in two variables) can be purposefully analyzed (with and without technology) to determine an efficient strategy to find a solution, if one exists, and then to justify the solution. ■ Know that finding solutions to an equation, inequality, or system of equations or inequalities requires the checking of candidate solutions, whether generated analytically or graphically, to ensure that solutions are found and that those found are not extraneous.

FIGURE 4.3, *continued*

Things to notice in Figure 4.3:

- The story of Integrated High School Mathematics 1 is about the study of patterns, from one-variable patterns in Unit 1 to two-variable patterns in Unit 2, and then on to the range of patterns of shape and of data in Units 3 and 4.

- As students study two-variable patterns in Unit 2, they examine different shapes of data, from linear functions with all their algebraic characteristics to an informal study of nonlinear patterns such as exponential and quadratic functions.

- Unit 3 studies the patterns in shape, introducing geometric patterns and constructions in one- and two-dimensional space, including properties and classifications of triangles, quadrilaterals, and circles. The transformations of such shapes lead to a study of congruence.

- Unit 4 turns to the patterns in chance as students study the probability of events in our world.

- Unit 5 concludes Integrated Math 1 with a capstone experience in which students study inequalities and linear programming, tying together linear inequalities, modeling, graphing, technology, and real-world applications.

Proposed Course Outline for Integrated High School Mathematics 2

Based on the big ideas, essential understandings, and proposed units in Figures 4.1 and 4.2, we propose the course outline for Integrated High School Mathematics 1 in Figure 4.4.

A PROPOSED COURSE OUTLINE FOR INTEGRATED HIGH SCHOOL MATHEMATICS 2		
UNIT	TOPICS	ESSENTIAL CONTENT
UNIT 1: Quadratic Functions and Models	■ Transformations of quadratic functions ■ Solving quadratic equations ■ Applications of quadratic functions	■ Understand that quadratic functions can be represented graphically, and key features of the graphs, including zeros, intercepts, and, when relevant, rate of change, and maximum/minimum values, can be associated with and interpreted in terms of the equivalent symbolic representation. ■ Use graphs to obtain exact or approximate solutions of equations, inequalities, and systems of equations and inequalities—including systems of linear equations in two variables and systems of linear and quadratic equations. ■ Understand that the structure of an equation or inequality can be purposefully analyzed to determine an efficient strategy to find a solution, if one exists, and then to justify the solution. ■ Recognize that expressions can be rewritten in equivalent forms by using algebraic properties, including properties of addition, multiplication, and exponentiation, to make different characteristics or features visible.

FIGURE 4.4

A PROPOSED COURSE OUTLINE FOR INTEGRATED HIGH SCHOOL MATHEMATICS 2, *cont.*

UNIT	TOPICS	ESSENTIAL CONTENT
UNIT 2: **Patterns in Space**	▪ Similarity and dilations ▪ Surface area and volume ▪ The Pythagorean theorem ▪ Right triangle trigonometry	▪ Understand that areas and volumes of figures can be computed by determining how the figure might be constructed from simpler figures by dissection and recombining. ▪ Recognize that when an object is the image of a known object under a similarity transformation, the length, area, or volume of the image can be computed by using proportional relationships. ▪ Understand that determining that two figures are similar involves finding a similarity transformation (dilation or composite of a dilation with a rigid motion) or, equivalently, a sequence of similarity transformations that maps one figure onto the other. ▪ Recognize congruence, similarity, symmetry, measurement opportunities, and other geometric ideas, including right triangle trigonometry in real-world contexts, provides a means of building understanding of these concepts. ▪ Use trigonometric ratios and the Pythagorean theorem to solve right triangles in applied problems.
UNIT 3: **Exponential Functions and Models**	▪ Rational exponents ▪ Representing exponential functions ▪ Interpreting and applying exponential functions	▪ Use the laws of exponents to interpret expressions for exponential functions using rational exponents. ▪ Understand that exponential functions can be represented graphically, and key features of the graphs, including zeros, intercepts, and, when relevant, rates of change and maximum/minimum values, can be associated with and interpreted in terms of equivalent symbolic representations. ▪ Use graphs to obtain exact or approximate solutions to exponential equations and systems of equations, including exponential equations.

FIGURE 4.4, *continued*   *continues*

A PROPOSED COURSE OUTLINE FOR INTEGRATED HIGH SCHOOL MATHEMATICS 2, *cont.*

UNIT	TOPICS	ESSENTIAL CONTENT
UNIT 4: Proofs, Inferences, and Data	• Inductive and deductive reasoning • Theorems about triangles and quadrilaterals and their proofs • Given a statement, construct a proof • Given a geometric diagram, propose conjectures and try to prove your conjectures • Randomness and variation in data	• Prove theorems about triangles, parallelograms, circles, coordinate geometry, congruence, and similarity. • Study designs of three main types: sample survey, experiment, and observational study. • Understand statistics as a process for making inferences about populations based on a random sample from that population. • Understand that the scope and validity of statistical inferences are dependent on the role of randomization in the study design. • Recognize the purposes of and differences among sample surveys, experiments, and observational studies, and explain how randomness relates to each. • Use data from sample surveys to estimate population means and from randomized experiments to compare two treatments and determine if differences between parameters are significant.
UNIT 5: Capstone: Quantitative Literacy: Using regression and correlation to analyze real data and build authentic models	• Regression and correlation to analyze real data and build authentic models	• Analyzing the association between two quantitative variables should involve statistical procedures, such as examining (with technology) the sum of squared deviations in fitting a linear model, analyzing residuals for patterns, generating a least-squares regression line and finding a correlation coefficient, and differentiating between correlation and causation. • Data-analysis techniques can be used to develop models of contextual situations and to generate and evaluate possible solutions to real problems involving those contexts. • Mathematical and statistical reasoning about data can be used to evaluate conclusions and assess risks. • Making and defending informed data-based decisions is a characteristic of a quantitatively literate person.

FIGURE 4.4, continued

Things to notice in Figure 4.4:

- Integrated High School Mathematics 2 includes a detailed look at nonlinear functions, including quadratics (Unit 1) and exponentials (Unit 3). These functions were explored from only an introductory perspective in grade 8 and Integrated Math I and are now analyzed using algebraic methods in one and two variables, including how they can be transformed, solved, and rewritten in different forms, and applied.

- Unit 2 continues our study of geometry, building on Unit 3 in Integrated Math I and expanding the study of shape to similarity and dilations, the Pythagorean theorem, right triangle trigonometry, and three-dimensional figures.

- In Unit 4, we move to inductive and deductive reasoning, including learning about proofs in geometry and inferences in statistics.

- The year concludes with our capstone unit, in which students will make and defend data-based decisions using statistical techniques.

Differentiation in Grades 9 and 10

We fully recognize that *differentiation* is an overused, and often misunderstood, word in education. Moreover, while many people talk about the need for more and better differentiation, few educators are clear on exactly what it means in practice in the classroom, particularly the mathematics classroom. We made our views clear in Chapter 3, where we said, "We start with the simple reality that there are plus or minus twenty-five distinct brains in every class of students. We add the obvious truism that 'one size never fits, doesn't fit, and can't ever fit all.' And we conclude that we can only maximize the learning of mathematics by differentiating." We went on to discuss how alternative approaches and multiple representations are two powerful ways of differentiating while teaching.

It is also incumbent upon us to recognize that meeting diverse student needs requires a broader notion of differentiation that entails enrichment, acceleration options, and boost-up opportunities.

Enrichment

All teaching and learning can be enriched with differentiated opportunities for extensions, deeper probes, projects, and independent study. It should be expected that all mathematics courses provide opportunities for supplemental enrichment that extend the required scope of any course. Such enrichment is an essential component of a detracked or more heterogeneous system. When planning and implementing the two common integrated courses described here, we urge teachers to draw from the broad array of online resources presented in Chapter 11 to provide ongoing opportunities for enriching and going deeper.

We have seen, and highly recommend, optional problems of the week, bonus tasks, and homework extensions that provide consistent platforms for enrichment.

Acceleration

We recognize that students come with differences in readiness for learning. Acceleration enables and encourages selected students to take the same coursework one or, in very rare cases, two years ahead of what is typical. That is, while the vast majority of students are likely to take a rigorous mathematics course in grade 8 and move on to the two Integrated High School Mathematics courses described above in grades 9 and 10, we fully recognize that some students can enter this sequence in grade 7 and can benefit from the opportunity to complete additional mathematics in grade 12.

In making these decisions, educators must ensure that accelerated opportunities are appropriate and no critical concepts are rushed or skipped. Moreover, any such acceleration should entail a deeper treatment of the *same* content a year earlier with room for additional enrichment and *not* a faster race to take more courses sooner. In this way, acceleration is an option for selected, highly capable students and not a different track with distinctly different potential outcomes. Decisions on exactly which students benefit from acceleration options and effective placement into these courses one year earlier than normal need to be collaboratively made by the mathematics department and the guidance department and thoroughly understood by all the members of both departments.

Boosting Up

Students often enter high school from many different schools, having had very diverse experiences and successes with mathematics. Given an effective middle school experience, most will be ready for the Integrated High School Mathematics 1 course we have proposed. In every school, however, for a wide variety of reasons, there will be high school freshmen who are *not* ready for the mathematics content and expectations of this course. We know that simply placing these students in this course without additional support essentially guarantees failure. We know that isolating these students in remedial courses and postponing this course for a year or two puts these students even further behind. And we know that teaching by more telling, showing, and practicing is not likely to suddenly switch on the "aha" light.

Accordingly, we urge high schools to adopt a double-period boost-up option for those students who, based on their eighth-grade grades and assessment data, are unlikely to succeed in this essential ninth-grade course. This is a model we have seen work with great success in the Howard County (MD) School District. The county designed a course called Algebra Seminar for approximately 20 percent of the ninth-grade class in each high school. These are students who are deemed unlikely to be able to pass the state test if they are enrolled in a typical one-period Algebra 1 class. In our case, an Integrated High School Mathematics 1 Seminar should be

- team-taught by a math teacher and a special education teacher

- systematically planned as a back-to-back double period

- capped at eighteen students

- supported with a common planning period made possible because Algebra Seminar teachers are limited to only four teaching periods

- supported with focused professional development

- composed of tasks and activities drawn from a broad array of print and nonprint resources

- noted for the variety of materials and resources used (such as graphing calculators, laptop computers, response clickers, and VersaTiles)

- enriched by a wide variety of highly effective instructional practices (including effective questioning, asking for explanations, and focusing on different representations and multiple approaches)

- supported by districtwide shared online lesson plans that teachers use to initiate their planning.

It should be clear that success in this proposed common integrated ninth-grade mathematics course is absolutely essential for continued success in high school mathematics. The expensive, but high-payoff, double-period option is one way to maximize the likelihood of a strong start leading to a strong finish for students.

Guiding Questions

1. What specifically and generally about the big ideas, essential understandings, proposed units of instruction, and course outlines for grades 9 and 10 mathematics do you find exciting and worth adopting? Why?

2. What specifically and generally about the big ideas, essential understandings, proposed units of instruction, and course outlines for grades 9 and 10 mathematics do you find scary or troublesome? Why?

3. What do you see as the greatest obstacles to moving your school or district toward a common, integrated set of two courses for grades 9 and 10 like what has been described in this chapter?

5

Let's make students' final required mathematical experience in high school more than a message that mathematics is abstract, hard, and irrelevant and not something a person will ever use.

—CATHY SEELEY (2019, 20)

Grades 11 and 12

Differentiated Pathways of Rigorous, Relevant Courses That Meet Real Student Needs

AS WE NOTED IN CHAPTER 1, among the challenges we face is the current reality of a single pathway through high school mathematics that ignores the diversity of post–high school needs and opportunities.

In Chapter 4, we proposed and defined a common, integrated curriculum of shared mathematical knowledge that we believe *all* ninth- and tenth-grade students both need and deserve. We turn now to the critical need to offer rigorous, relevant differentiated pathways for the last two years of high school that far more appropriately link high school to post–high school life and needs.

Beyond Algebra 2: The Need for Change

In a rare display of agreement (see Figure 5.1), nearly every major mathematical society and organization has stated that curriculum change in mathematics (in high school and college) is desperately needed and past due.

With the best of intentions, and based on a serious conflation of correlation and causality, policy makers and guidance counselors have used the fact that students who successfully complete the Algebra 2 obstacle course are more likely to attend college as a justification for expecting or requiring it as a rite of passage. Twenty states require students to take Algebra 2 or Integrated Math 3 (Achieve 2020).

A CONSENSUS ACROSS ORGANIZATIONS

American Mathematical Association of Two-Year Colleges (AMATYC 2014)	The equivalent content in intermediate algebra courses is not required to master the content for most college-level mathematics courses that do not lead to calculus.
Mathematical Association of America (Saxe and Braddy 2015, 13)	The current attention to big data and the demand for college graduates with data skills should prompt changes in our entry-level courses. . . . Thus, there is a call to provide mathematically substantive options for students who are not headed to calculus. These entry courses should focus on problem solving, modeling, statistics, and applications.
National Council of Teachers of Mathematics (NCTM 2018)	The answer to these challenges is not, as some would argue, simply to require less mathematics; rather, it is necessary to identify, confront, and make long over-due changes to the structures, policies, instructional approaches, and focus and relevance of high school mathematics.
The President's Council of Advisors on Science and Technology (PCAST 2012)	Outdated course materials and teaching techniques have not provided students with the quantitative skills demanded for employment and good citizenship.

FIGURE 5.1

Algebra 2 usually involves pencil-and-paper solution methods for various types of equations and the study of quadratic, exponential, rational, polynomial, and radical functions. Historically, its purpose was to prepare students to study calculus, but because of its failure to do so, a Precalculus course was developed to include a more intensive study of functions. We are left today with an Algebra 2 course that moves from a review of Algebra 1 to the "thrills" of quadratic, radical, rational, and polynomial functions that represent, for many students, their final ugly high school mathematics experience.

Cathy Seeley (2019) argues:

> Unfortunately, our well-intentioned—and long overdue—attention to inequities in student placement has resulted in creating new inequities. Now, all students have the opportunity to experience the same level of high school rigor. But that opportunity is subverted by schools clinging to outdated courses that do not serve

all students well. Algebra II is the prime example of such a course, with students struggling just to pass, even if they do so without understanding, and with some students dropping out of school or diverting their future path solely because they haven't been able to succeed in the irrelevant content of Algebra II. (18–19)

As an alternative to the fiction that mastery of Algebra 2 is a prerequisite for success in college and careers, we offer the research of the National Center on Education and the Economy (NCEE 2013) that debunks this notion. This research has found that the most demanding mathematics in courses generally required of college students is typically the content associated with Algebra 1, some limited Algebra 2 content, and a few topics in Geometry, and thus one cannot make the case that all high school graduates must be proficient in Algebra 2 to be ready for college and careers. Moreover, when only about 15 percent of any age cohort go on to STEM majors, we know that most American workers will never need to master much of what has passed for Algebra 2.

More Than Algebra 2 Can Be Rigorous

Let's make no mistake: the pressure to keep Algebra 2 as the gatekeeping hurdle it has become is grounded in the commonly held assumption that Algebra 2 is more "rigorous" than other, alternative mathematics course options. We believe that *rigor* is one of those words bandied around to sound impressive, but usually doesn't mean much more than "more challenging." This incorrect assumption allows Algebra 2 to stand proxy for rigor in the high school mathematics curriculum and creates the impression that other mathematics courses are thus not as rigorous. It also creates a false dichotomy that students either are in a rigorous pathway toward Calculus or are not taking rigorous courses.

In academic subjects other than mathematics, rigor typically refers not to the content but to the expectations for, and quality of, student work. Any alternative to Algebra 2 can and must use this more common definition of rigor. We know that the Statistics AP examination is no less rigorous than the Calculus AB and BC examinations. We know that we can teach topics in financial literacy, for example, why paying the minimum balance on a credit card bill is a losing proposition, in a very rigorous, yet accessible, manner.

Rather than focusing on the development of algebraic manipulations in preparation for calculus, a set of coherent, relevant, and alternative pathways for grades 11 and 12 can be equally rigorous, but with different goals and purposes. We strongly believe that these alternative, differentiated pathways should do the following:

- Focus on sense-making, authentic use and modeling, data analysis, computational thinking, and using functions to reason through and tackle unfamiliar problems.

- Require students to make decisions based on analysis of messy, uncertain situations.

- Include challenging, meaningful, and relevant tasks, most of which require the use of technological tools.

- Emphasize the importance, relevance, and application of mathematics for solving real-world problems. That is, [teach] students to understand important mathematics deeply. Rather than increasing the mathematical complexity by taking students through more and more abstract and disconnected manipulations, the [courses should teach] application of mathematical concepts in increasingly complex situations. (Charles A. Dana Center 2020, 40)

Phil Daro and Harold Asturias (2019) add that designing new math pathways can accomplish at least four important goals:

1. Students will be able to learn the mathematics that prepares them for STEM careers.

2. Students will be able to learn the mathematics that prepares them for [other] careers without being blocked by irrelevant requirements.

3. Latinx and African American students will have ample opportunities to thrive in college, including in STEM fields, as will female students of all ethnicities.

4. Students who initially choose a [non-STEM] pathway will be able to switch to a STEM pathway during high school or college, and vice versa, if their interests change. (8)

These are the widely shared goals of nearly all teachers of mathematics, and the rigorous, relevant, differentiated pathways for which we argue in the rest of this chapter attempt to meet these goals.

Pathways for Grades 11–12

High school pathways should create equitable opportunities that connect mathematics to students' goals and interests and ensure equitable and evidence-based instruction. Any pathway design must account for

- creating rigorous pathways that articulate with postsecondary policies and practices and align with a range of student aspirations

- giving more weight to student aspirations and less to students' perceived preparation levels

- supporting educators to address the role of bias and privilege in traditional school structures and to dislodge harmful preconceptions about student abilities

- implementing instructional and support strategies that address uneven prior opportunities and damaged math student identities

- ensuring that pathway options are communicated early, publicly, and clearly to all stakeholders

- establishing summer or semester courses to serve as bridges for students who choose to switch pathways (Daro and Asturias 2019).

Accordingly, building on important work of the Charles A. Dana Center at the University of Texas at Austin (2020) and the emerging proposals from Georgia, Ohio, Oregon, and Alabama, we offer the following structure for invigorating and expanding opportunities in high school mathematics (see Figure 5.2).

A FRAMEWORK FOR INVIGORATED HIGH SCHOOL MATHEMATICS

GRADE	COURSES		
9	Integrated High School Mathematics 1		
10	Integrated High School Mathematics 2		
	Quantitative Literacy Pathway	**Statistics Pathway**	**Calculus Pathway**
11	The mathematics of real-world problem solving, modeling, financial literacy, and effective citizenship: students intending to follow paths in technical fields, liberal arts, and communications	The mathematics of data, uncertainty, and chance: students intending to enter health, social science, and business fields	The mathematics of functions and change: students intending to enter STEM and natural science fields
12	A range of fourth-year math options, including AP Statistics, Introduction to Data Science, Financial Mathematics, Mathematical Modeling, or Discrete Mathematics		Precalculus or Calculus or AP Calculus or AP Statistics

FIGURE 5.2

Why Three Pathways?

Some states appear to be moving to two pathways—one traditional and one nontraditional. However, many colleges and universities appear to be moving toward three freshman-year pathways—one quantitative and preparatory for the humanities and technical fields, one statistical and preparatory for the social sciences, and one heavily symbolic and calculus oriented that is preparatory for the natural sciences and STEM fields. We have taken our cue from these three pathways.

What the Pathways Have in Common

- **Technology:** The pathways must make full use of technologies that increase the productivity of instruction and enrich students' experiences. The use of calculators, computers, data-gathering tools and probes, interactive software, and student response systems should be pervasive throughout instruction and assessment.

- **Problem solving and reasoning:** The goal of each pathway is for students to develop a deep understanding of mathematical concepts and principles. Students must be able to ask penetrating questions, explain their thinking, make reasonable estimates and predictions, and justify and respond to one another's mathematical arguments, strategies, and decisions.

- **Rigor:** In each pathway, the expectations are high for student work and the course teaches students to understand important mathematics deeply.

- **Modeling:** Each pathway must include the uses of numeric, algebraic, geometric, and statistical ideas to model, better understand, and more accurately explain real-world situations and phenomena.

The Quantitative Literacy Pathway

The quantitative literacy pathway focuses on the mathematics of numbers, modeling, financial literacy, and effective citizenship. Quantitative literacy (QL) is often defined as the ability to understand and use numbers and data analyses in everyday life. Lynn Steen, way back in 1997, warned that "an innumerate citizen today is as vulnerable as the illiterate peasant of Gutenberg's time" (628). This is even more true today, more than twenty years later. Addressing health concerns, understanding government decisions and political arguments, making smart financial and investment decisions: all these require quantitative literacy.

Contrary to popular belief, only a small part of what is commonly referred to as quantitative literacy is adequately developed in school mathematics. Once basic arithmetic is covered, the curriculum moves on to advanced and abstract algebraic mathematical concepts, and students seldom gain experiences in applying quantitative skills in subtle but sophisticated real-world contexts. For example, lessons in a Quantitative Reasoning course might uncover the accessible, yet still rigorous, mathematics of how FICO scores are generated or ask students to examine the data on U.S. incarceration rates as compared to the rest of the world and write up their findings in a report. Figure 5.3 shows a proposed course outline for an eleventh-grade Quantitative Reasoning course as an entry to this pathway.

QUANTITATIVE REASONING (QR)

The Charles A. Dana Center at The University of Texas at Austin convened national experts in quantitative reasoning courses to develop the following college-level QR learning outcomes (2016, xx–xxiii). We propose the learning outcomes also represent the priority instructional content for a high school QR course.

UNIT 1: **Number, Ratio, and Proportional Reasoning**	■ Solve real-life problems requiring interpretation and comparison of various representations of ratios (i.e., fractions, decimals, rates, and percentages). ■ Demonstrate procedural fluency with real number arithmetic operations and use those operations to represent real-world scenarios and to solve stated problems. ■ Demonstrate number sense, including dimensional analysis and conversions between fractions, decimals, and percentages. Determine when approximations are appropriate and when exact calculations are necessary.
UNIT 2: **Modeling**	■ Analyze and critique mathematical models and be able to describe their limitations. ■ Use models, including models created with spreadsheets or other tools, to estimate solutions to contextual questions, identify patterns, and identify how changing parameters affect the results. ■ Choose and create models for bivariate data sets, and use the models to answer questions and draw conclusions or make decisions. ■ Solve linear equations, graph and interpret linear models, and read and apply formulas.

FIGURE 5.3   *continues*

QUANTITATIVE REASONING (QR), *cont.*	
UNIT 3: **Probability**	▪ Evaluate claims based on empirical, theoretical, and subjective probabilities. ▪ Use data displays and models to determine probabilities (including conditional probabilities) and use these probabilities to make informed decisions.
UNIT 4: **Statistics**	▪ Use statistical information from studies, surveys, and polls (including when reported in condensed form or as summary statistics) to make informed decisions. ▪ Create and use visual displays of data. ▪ Summarize, represent, and interpret data sets on a single count or measurement variable. ▪ Demonstrate a basic understanding of displays of univariate data such as bar graphs, histograms, dotplots, and circle graphs, including appropriate labeling. ▪ Use properties of distributions to analyze data and answer questions. ▪ Solve real-life problems requiring interpretation and comparison of complex numerical summaries that extend beyond simple measures of center.

More information on the Dana Center's QR course is available at www.utdanacenter.org/our-work/higher-education /curricular-resources-higher-education/quantitative-reasoning.

FIGURE 5.3, continued

The Statistics Pathway

The statistics pathway focuses on the mathematics of data, uncertainty, and chance and is aimed especially at students with an interest in health, social sciences, and business.

According to Jo Boaler (2019), "The answer is as obvious as it is radical: to put data and its analysis at the center of high school mathematics. Every high school student should graduate with an understanding of data, spreadsheets, and the difference between correlation and causality."

Thus in 2013, Introduction to Data Science (IDS) was created by UCLA in partnership with the Los Angeles Unified School District (LAUSD). The IDS curriculum was created under the auspices of the National Science Foundation's Mathematics and Science Partnership grant, "MOBILIZE: Mobilizing for Innovative Computer Science Teaching and Learning." LAUSD secured approval from the University of California to recognize IDS as a statistics course that provides students with another option besides Algebra 2 in the college pathway. IDS is designed to develop students' computational and statistical thinking skills. Computationally, students learn to write code to enhance analyses of data, to break large problems into smaller pieces, and to understand and employ algorithms to solve problems. Statistical thinking skills include developing a data "habit of mind" in which one learns to seek data to answer questions or support (or undermine) claims; thinking critically about the ability of particular data to support claims; learning to interpret analyses of data; and learning to communicate findings. The purpose of IDS is to introduce students to dynamic data analysis (see Figure 5.4).

INTRODUCTION TO DATA SCIENCE (IDS)

The standards listed in this figure name the priority instructional content for a high school data science course.

UNIT 1: **The Idea of Data**	▪ Represent data with plots on the real number line (dot plots, histograms, and box plots). ▪ Use statistics appropriate to the shape of the data distribution to compare center (median, mean) of two or more different data sets (measures of spread will be studied in Unit 2). ▪ Interpret differences in shape, center, and spread in the context of the data sets, accounting for possible effects of extreme data points (outliers). ▪ Summarize categorical data for two categories in two-way frequency tables. Interpret relative frequencies in the context of the data (joint, marginal, and conditional relative frequencies). Recognize possible associations and trends in the data. ▪ Represent data on two quantitative variables on a scatterplot, and describe how the variables are related. ▪ Evaluate reports based on data.
UNIT 2: **Making Inferences, Justifying Conclusions, and Probability**	▪ Use statistics appropriate to the shape of the data distribution to compare center (median, mean) and spread (interquartile range, standard deviation) of two or more different data sets. ▪ Interpret differences in shape, center, and spread in the context of the data sets, accounting for possible effects of extreme data points (outliers). ▪ Use the mean and standard deviation of a data set to fit it to a normal distribution and to estimate population percentages. Understand that there are data sets for which such a procedure is not appropriate. Use calculators, spreadsheets, and tables to estimate areas under the normal curve. ▪ Decide if a specified model is consistent with results from a given data-generating process, e.g., using simulation. ▪ Evaluate reports based on data. ▪ Understand that two events A and B are independent if the probability of A and B occurring together is the product of their probabilities, and use this characterization to determine if they are independent. ▪ Use permutations to perform [informal] inference.

FIGURE 5.4　　　　　　　　　　　　　　　　　　　　　　*continues*

INTRODUCTION TO DATA SCIENCE (IDS), *cont.*

UNIT 3: Data Collection Methods	▪ Understand statistics as a process for making inferences about population parameters based on a random sample from that population. ▪ Recognize the purposes of and differences among sample surveys, experiments, and observational studies; explain how randomization relates to each. ▪ Evaluate reports based on data.
UNIT 4: Algebra	▪ Decide if a specified model is consistent with results from a given data-generating process, e.g., using simulation. ▪ Represent data on two quantitative variables on a scatterplot, and describe how the variables are related. ▪ Fit a function to the data; use functions fitted to data to solve problems in the context of the data. Use given functions or choose a function suggested by the context. ▪ Informally assess the fit of a function by plotting and analyzing residuals. ▪ Fit a linear function for a scatterplot that suggests a linear association. ▪ Interpret the slope (rate of change) and the intercept (constant term) of a linear model in the context of the data. ▪ Compute (using technology) and interpret the correlation coefficient of a linear fit. ▪ Evaluate reports based on data.

Source: Gould, R., S. Machado, T. Johnson, and J. Molyneux. 2015. Introduction to Data Science. This work is licensed under the Creative Commons Attribution-ShareAlike 4.0 International License (http://creativecommons.org/licenses/by-sa/4.0).

FIGURE 5.4, *continued*

IDS emphasizes the use of statistics and computation as tools for creative work, and as a means of telling stories with data. Seen in this way, its content prepares students to "read" and think critically about existing data stories. Ultimately, this course is about how to discern good stories from bad through a practice that involves compiling evidence from one or more sources, and which often requires hands-on examination of one or more data sets. IDS develops the tools, techniques, and principles for reasoning about the world with data. It presents a process that is iterative and authentically inquiry based, comparing multiple "views" of one or more data sets. The full IDS curriculum is available for download at www.introdatascience.org /introduction-to-data-science-curriculum.

The Calculus Pathway

The calculus pathway focuses on the mathematics of functions and leads to calculus. It is appropriate for students aiming toward STEM careers.

The whole purpose of three equivalently rigorous differentiated pathways is to provide options other than Algebra 2 and Precalculus for most students while preserving the power, beauty, and importance of much of the traditional Algebra 2 and Precalculus content for students for whom symbolic, algebraic, calculus-driven mathematics aligns with their inclinations and future plans. But that does not mean Algebra 2 and Precalculus can or should be replicated essentially unchanged from the content of traditional courses, while continuing to prepare students for the equivalent of AP Calculus AB or BC in high school for accelerated students and freshman-year college calculus for others.

In thinking through the content and organization of a grade 11 Intermediate High School Algebra course, we build directly from the proposed common integrated courses for grades 9 and 10 described in Chapter 4 and make the following design assumptions:

- Intermediate High School Algebra continues the progressions of the mathematics of functions begun in grade 8 and continued in Integrated High School Mathematics 1 and 2.

- While many students in this course will likely stay within the pathway and continue directly on to Calculus, for others this is likely to be a precursor to AP Statistics or one of the courses in either the quantitative literacy or statistics pathway.

- Since so much of the traditional Precalculus curriculum is about readiness for what is essentially a pencil-and-paper Calculus course still driven by the demands of the Calculus AP examinations, our thinking is that, until the AP exam changes for the better, Intermediate High School Algebra needs to focus much more on models of functions, applications, and the use of technology than is currently common, leaving some of the symbol manipulation to Calculus itself during grade 12.

- One way to accomplish this goal of focusing on models and applications with the support of technology is to downplay or eliminate the emphasis on rational expressions and rational functions. Several other legacy topics could easily be eliminated, such as Cramer's rule, Descartes' rule of signs, the rational root theorem, and synthetic division. Historically, these were valuable tools of the mathematician, but given today's technology, locating the real roots of a polynomial is no longer a challenge. But understanding what the roots are and knowing how to use them are critical.

Figure 5.5 shows a set of units and topics for this course.

UNITS AND TOPICS FOR GRADE 11 INTERMEDIATE HIGH SCHOOL ALGEBRA

The standards listed in this table name the priority instructional content for an Intermediate Algebra course.

UNIT 1: **Series and** **Sequences**	■ Use physical and visual models and algebraic formulas to represent and analyze sequences and series. ■ Develop an informal notion of limit (converging and diverging series and sequences). ■ Link arithmetic series with linear functions and link geometric series with exponential functions. ■ Derive and apply formulas for given terms and sums of arithmetic and geometric sequences and series. ■ Examine patterns and applications of triangular numbers, Fibonacci numbers, the golden mean, and Pascal's triangle.
UNIT 2: **Functions,** **Inverse** **Functions, and** **Transformations**	■ Use modeling, applications, and technology to review the work on functions done in Integrated High School Mathematics 1 and 2. ■ Write functions in different but equivalent forms to reveal and explain different properties of the functions. ■ Combine functions by addition, subtraction, multiplication, and division to build new functions. ■ Determine the composition of two functions, including any necessary restrictions on the domain. ■ Describe the conditions under which an inverse relation is a function. ■ Determine and graph the inverse relation of a function, and relate functions and their inverses to transformations.
UNIT 3: **More Nonlinear** **Functions—** **Logarithms,** **Absolute Value,** **and Piecewise**	■ Solve equations and inequalities involving the absolute value of a linear expression. ■ Determine key characteristics of absolute value, step, and other piecewise-defined functions. ■ Recognize, express, and solve problems that can be modeled using absolute value, step, and other piecewise-defined functions. Interpret their solutions in terms of the context. ■ Recognize, express, and solve problems that can be modeled using exponential functions, including those for which logarithms provide an efficient method of solution. Interpret their solutions in terms of the context. ■ Translate between exponential and logarithmic forms. ■ Use technology to graph and solve exponential and logarithmic equations and their applications. ■ Understand the number e.

FIGURE 5.5

UNITS AND TOPICS FOR GRADE 11
INTERMEDIATE HIGH SCHOOL ALGEBRA, *cont.*

UNIT 4: **Complex Numbers, Radical and Rational Equations, and Functions**	- Represent complex numbers in the form $a + bi$, where a and b are real; simplify powers of pure imaginary numbers. - Solve single-variable quadratic equations and inequalities over the complex numbers; graph real solution sets on a number line. - Solve single-variable quadratic, exponential, rational, radical, and factorable higher-order polynomial equations over the set of real numbers, including quadratic equations involving absolute value. - Use the discriminant to determine the nature of the solutions of the equation. - Determine key characteristics of simple rational and radical functions and their graphs. - Represent simple rational and radical functions using tables, graphs, verbal statements, and equations. Translate among these representations. - Perform operations on rational expressions, including complex fractions.
UNIT 5: **Polynomial Equations, Functions, and End Behavior**	- Perform operations on polynomial expressions. - Determine key characteristics of power functions in the form for positive integral values of n and their graphs. - Determine key characteristics of polynomial functions and their graphs. - Examine end behavior of functions. - Represent polynomial functions using tables, graphs, verbal statements, and equations. Translate among these representations. - Use real or realistic data, either given or collected, to create and analyze the appropriateness of models.
UNIT 6: **Trigonometric Functions and Models**	- Relate angle measure in degrees and radians. - Explain and show how the unit circle extends trigonometric functions to all real numbers. - Use special triangles to mentally determine the sine, cosine, and tangent of $\frac{\pi}{3}$, $\frac{\pi}{4}$, and $\frac{\pi}{6}$, and use the unit circle to express the values of sine, cosine, and tangent for $\pi - x$, $\pi + x$, and $2\pi - x$ in terms of their values for any real number x. - Model periodic phenomena with trigonometric functions given an amplitude, frequency, and midline. - Use inverse functions to solve trigonometric equations and evaluate and interpret these solutions. - Prove the Pythagorean identity and use it to find the sine, cosine, or tangent given the value of one of these ratios and the quadrant of the angle. - Prove and apply the laws of sines and the law of cosines.

FIGURE 5.5, *continued*

continues

UNITS AND TOPICS FOR GRADE 11
INTERMEDIATE HIGH SCHOOL ALGEBRA, *cont.*

UNIT 7: Modeling with Functions	■ Mathematically proficient students can apply the mathematics they know to solve problems arising in everyday life, society, and the workplace. A student might use geometry to solve a design problem or use a function to describe how one quantity of interest depends on another. Mathematically proficient students who can apply what they know are comfortable making assumptions and approximations to simplify a complicated situation, realizing that these may need revision later. They are able to identify important quantities in a practical situation and map their relationships using such tools as diagrams, two-way tables, graphs, flowcharts, and formulas. They can analyze those relationships mathematically to draw conclusions. They routinely interpret their mathematical results in the context of the situation and reflect on whether the results make sense, possibly improving the model if it has not served its purpose. (Adapted from National Governors Association Center for Best Practices, Council of Chief State School Officers 2010.) For specific suggestions, see Chapters 9 and 11.

FIGURE 5.5, *continued*

Things to notice about the Intermediate High School Algebra course outlined in Figure 5.5:

■ We make a deliberate connection and mathematical bridging from the Integrated High School Mathematics 2 course outlined in Chapter 4 to this Intermediate High School Algebra course that blends and consolidates key aspects of typical Algebra 2 and Precalculus. We believe that these units provide a critical balance between consolidating previously introduced mathematical ideas and introducing new mathematical ideas that extend the work of grades 9 and 10, but with a more abstract and symbolic focus. Given what we have seen in schools adopting such a three-year integrated sequence, many of these students should be ready to take Calculus in grade 12 *without resorting to acceleration along the way.*

■ As was the case with the courses outlined in Chapter 4, we have tried to honor the scope principle that "less is more" and that slowing down the rush through content is essential to shift the focus to deeper understanding, application, modeling, and justification. That is why this proposed replacement for Algebra 2 is limited to seven units, each expected to take from five to six weeks, giving teacher *and* students, with one hour of mathematics each day and the significant incorporation of technology, the needed time to move far beyond memorization and symbol manipulation.

- A broad range of resources are provided in Chapter 11 from which relevant and engaging tasks and problems can be selected.

- The focus of each of the proposed units should be on big ideas, applications, and modeling—all with the consistent assistance of online graphing calculators. We urge teachers to approach these algebraic topics by presenting problems (like geometrical diagrams or sets of data) and asking questions like

  - What do you notice?

  - What do you wonder?

  - What is going on here?

  - How might we represent this situation?

  - What questions might a normal human being be interested in answering based on this situation?

  - So, what did we learn by doing this work?

- Technology allows us to reduce a good deal of the symbol manipulation currently found in Algebra 2, including such essentially obsolete topics as rationalizing denominators, synthetic division, factoring polynomials of degree greater than or equal to 3, trigonometric identities, and graphing by hand (as opposed to just sketching).

- We believe that beginning this course with series and sequences enables the use of a wide variety of visual patterns, focuses on generalization, and allows for a powerful review of linear, quadratic, and exponential functions.

- Finally, just as we proposed a unifying capstone unit on Inequalities and Linear Programming in Integrated High School Mathematics 1 and on data in Integrated High School Mathematics 2 to end the year with content that communicates the power and applicability of mathematics, we propose that Intermediate High School Algebra end the year with a Modeling with Functions unit designed to provide every student with a range of experiences that show the power and utility of the mathematics learned in high school.

Options for Grade 12

The final year of high school mathematics could offer students a variety of possible courses in addition to the traditional Calculus pipeline. Alternatives include AP Statistics, Financial Mathematics, History of Mathematics, Mathematical Modeling, or Discrete Mathematics. Other innovative courses that address students' interests and future needs, such as mathematics for computer science, for other technology careers, or for fine arts, should also be considered, as long as they provide students with nonterminal, meaningful mathematics learning (NCTM 2018). In Alabama, in the fourth year of mathematics, students select one or more specialized courses that prepare them for future success in the postsecondary study of mathematics and in careers. The fourth-year courses are designed to prepare students for credit-bearing postsecondary study of mathematics and other future mathematical needs. Working backward from a desired field of study or profession, students can identify what their postsecondary needs may be and then determine which specialized fourth-year course might best prepare them to reach their future goals.

Pathways versus Tracking

In this new world of parallel options or pathways, students are offered options based on their own aspirations and interests. With appropriate guidance and information, students implementing their own choices may work harder than students who have been simply assigned to a course. If the best way to ensure that students have genuine opportunities to prepare for their futures is by offering multiple math pathways, who decides which pathway a student pursues, and when should that choice be made? This is a difficult and important question.

Ideally, the decision should be made in high school after two years of our proposed Integrated High School Mathematics sequence. In the past, and often the present, students' options frequently have been limited by tracking policies, as well as by inadequate course offerings, with decisions being made for students by counselors and teachers but rarely in transparent ways. Let's be clear again: Existing high school math sequences, and the way students are traditionally assigned to them, are part of the problem. They are based on the presumption of one primary pathway toward Calculus in which only some students can succeed (Daro and Asturias 2019). Given that the most practical time for pathways to diverge is after tenth grade, a student decision tree (see Figure 5.6) is crucial for *students* to select a pathway after tenth grade based on their future career and/or collegiate path in consultation with their parents, teachers, and counselors.

Teachers, parents, and counselors will have to actively support students in developing STEM aspirations and recruiting students from racial, ethnic, gender, or social class groups not well represented in STEM. Moreover, students who initially opt for a non-STEM pathway must have the opportunity to switch to a STEM pathway during

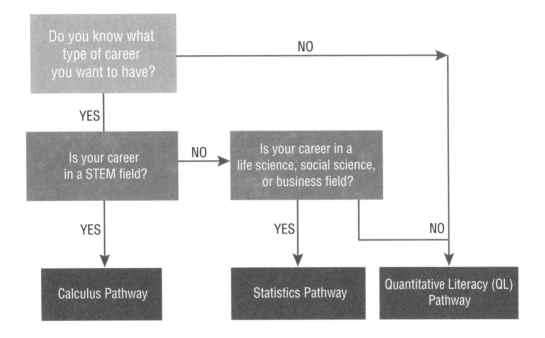

FIGURE 5.6 Pathway Decision Tree

high school and vice versa, if and when their interests change. Changing from one pathway to another will be more successful since all students will have had experiences with rigorous mathematics instead of the shallow survey courses that are currently often the alternative.

Acceleration Option

As noted in Chapter 4, educators must ensure that accelerated opportunities are appropriate and available only to mathematically exceptional students. No critical concepts should be rushed or skipped, as often happens with students who are currently accelerated into Algebra 1 in seventh or eighth grades. Figure 5.7 shows both the Standard Sequence as well as an Accelerated Sequence for the Calculus Pathway. The Accelerated Sequence would allow for a deeper treatment of the content a year earlier with room for additional enrichment, rather than represent entirely different courses that prematurely limit the options for students who are not accelerated.

A FRAMEWORK FOR THE CALCULUS TRACK OPTIONS

GRADE	STANDARD SEQUENCE	ACCELERATED SEQUENCE
8	Grade 8 Mathematics	Integrated High School Mathematics 1
9	Integrated High School Mathematics 1	Integrated High School Mathematics 2
10	Intermediate High School Mathematics 2	Integrated High School Algebra
11	Intermediate High School Algebra	AP Calculus
12	AP Calculus	AP Statistics or other advanced course

FIGURE 5.7

Conclusion

Teachers of high school mathematics know and understand the problems and challenges with the monolithic, single-pathway system that has been imposed on them. Teachers also understand the power of tradition, the wrath of angry parents who want for their children exactly what they believe helped them become successful, and the maddening cry of "But it's on the test!" But teachers also understand that while the traditional Algebra 2 and Precalculus courses may have been entirely appropriate for *some* students, they are *not* meeting the needs of the majority of high school juniors and seniors, and that the time has come to consider a system of alternative rigorous, yet relevant, courses allocated to three distinct pathways.

Guiding Questions

1. What specifically and generally about the courses and pathways proposed for grades 11 and 12 mathematics do you find exciting and worth adopting? Why?

2. What specifically and generally about the courses and pathways proposed for grades 11 and 12 mathematics do you find scary or troublesome? Why?

3. What do you see as the greatest obstacles to moving your school or district toward a differentiated set of pathways for grades 11 and 12 like what has been described in this chapter? What might to done to reduce these obstacles?

Part 3

What Invigorated Math Must Look Like

For too long, high school mathematics courses have been determined by a single textbook. The lessons in the text governed our pedagogy. The lesson examples determined the balance of skills, concepts, and applications. The chapter tests informed our assessments. And there was little guidance on the uses of technology or the incorporation of modeling.

We know with great certainty that the changes in the curriculum described in Part 2 can be implemented effectively only when we make equivalent shifts in our pedagogy, our assessments, and the use of technology, and make modeling a key component of high school mathematics.

The table below captures the three critical aspects of teaching and learning using different lenses. But as a whole, this table reminds us all that simply answering the question "What should we teach?" is insufficient to change teaching and learning.

THREE CORE INTERCONNECTED ASPECTS OF TEACHING AND LEARNING

SHORT QUESTION	EDUCATIONAL ASPECT	ACTION	EXTENDED QUESTION
What?	Curriculum	Planning	What content do we expect students to learn?
How?	Instruction	Implementing	How do we expect teachers to orchestrate instruction?
How well?	Assessment	Evaluating	How do we know that we have been successful, and if not, what must be done to remedy this?

Accordingly, the four chapters of Part 3 are filled with examples that give us a glimpse of what teaching, assessment, use of technology, and mathematical modeling should look like throughout an invigorated high school mathematics program.

6

*We now know that much of the problem rests
with an outdated mode of instruction, a lecture format
in which students are reduced to scribes.*

—DAVID BRESSOUD (2018)

Pedagogy

*We Know What Equitable
and Empowering Teaching Looks Like*

THE CHANGES IN CURRICULUM that we have outlined in Chapters 4 and 5 are a necessary, but insufficient, first step. Without accompanying changes in pedagogy, they will make little difference in students disposition toward mathematics or their learning. Successful change in high school mathematics will require transforming how mathematics is taught and facing our own individual and collective roles in changing a system that does not currently serve all students well. We recognize how challenging it is to change teaching practice and therefore devote this chapter to describing specific strategies and techniques, along with offering examples, that can make significant differences in student learning and disposition.

We believe that all teachers can facilitate student success in mathematics, and we cannot underestimate the power of the environment in our classrooms to positively influence student learning. For example, consider the tasks we choose to support learning. We can require endless practice on worksheet exercises, or we can select rich and engaging tasks that actually elicit student comments like "That was really cool." Or consider the questions we ask our students. We can focus on "How?" and "What's next?" or we can regularly ask students "Why?" or "Can you convince us?" We can assume, usually foolishly, that since we taught it, most of them learned it, or we can use and apply exit tickets to formatively assess learning and actually gather and use evidence of learning or the lack thereof.

It is unfortunate, however, that many parents and even some educators believe that students should be taught as they were taught, through memorizing facts, formulas, and procedures and then practicing skills over and over again. This view perpetuates the traditional lesson paradigm that features review, demonstration, and practice and is still pervasive in many classrooms (Banilower et al. 2006; Weiss and Pasley 2004). Thus, it is extremely clear that mathematics instruction and pedagogy stand at a crossroads. Surprisingly and powerfully, even the Mathematical Association of America (2015) challenges all mathematics educators to gather the courage to try actively engaging students with student-centered instructional strategies to fulfill our professional responsibility to our students.

To underscore these statements, in a 2008 survey of high school mathematics teachers, nearly 90 percent of survey respondents gave high or medium priority to actions that would transform traditional instructional practice into independent, collaborative, and whole-class work on significant mathematical and applied problems as the predominant activity in high school mathematics classes. Similar numbers endorsed the propositions that calculators and computers should be a regular presence in the high school mathematics classroom and that aspects of mathematical thinking like strategic competence, adaptive reasoning, productive disposition, and communication of ideas should also be the explicit foci of classroom activity and discussion (National Mathematics Advisory Panel 2008b).

To identify and exemplify the pedagogical changes necessary, this chapter draws from the eight mathematics teaching practices as defined and described in NCTM's *Principles to Actions* (2014) to help us craft a vision of mathematics classrooms (see Figure 6.1).

What is so refreshing about these eight practices is that they remind us that, based on common sense, the wisdom of practice, *and* research, we know what works and what needs to be found in every classroom in which mathematics is taught. The elaborations on each practice found in *Principles to Actions* describe exactly what students, teachers, and leaders should be doing, as well as what doesn't work and shouldn't be practiced. However, in many high school mathematics classrooms, students are still passively engaged with mathematics, and little mathematical discourse occurs. Moreover, mathematics is positioned as having little relevance to students' lives or experiences. How students are positioned to participate in mathematics affects not only what they learn but also how they come to see themselves as learners. The ways in which students view themselves as learners of mathematics greatly influence how they participate (Bishop 2012; Nasir and Hand 2006). Developing students' identities should be part of teachers' daily work, in which they use teaching practices that engage students, leverage multiple mathematical competencies, affirm mathematical identities, challenge marginality, and draw on multiple resources of knowledge (Aguirre, Mayfield-Ingram, and Martin 2013).

MATHEMATICS TEACHING PRACTICES

Establish mathematics goals to focus learning. Effective teaching of mathematics establishes clear goals for the mathematics that students are learning, situates goals within learning progressions, and uses the goals to guide instructional decisions.

Implement tasks that promote reasoning and problem solving. Effective teaching of mathematics engages students in solving and discussing tasks that promote mathematical reasoning and problem solving and allow multiple entry points and varied solution strategies.

Use and connect mathematical representations. Effective teaching of mathematics engages students in making connections among mathematical representations to deepen understanding of mathematics concepts and procedures as tools for problem solving.

Facilitate meaningful mathematical discourse. Effective teaching of mathematics facilitates discourse among students to build shared understanding of mathematical ideas by analyzing and comparing student approaches and arguments.

Pose purposeful questions. Effective teaching of mathematics uses purposeful questions to assess and advance students' reasoning and sense making about important mathematical ideas and relationships.

Build procedural fluency from conceptual understanding. Effective teaching of mathematics builds fluency with procedures on a foundation of conceptual understanding so that students, over time, become skillful in using procedures flexibly as they solve contextual and mathematical problems.

Support productive struggle in learning mathematics. Effective teaching of mathematics consistently provides students, individually and collectively, with opportunities and supports to engage in productive struggle as they grapple with mathematical ideas and relationships.

Elicit and use evidence of student thinking. Effective teaching of mathematics uses evidence of student thinking to assess progress toward mathematical understanding and to adjust instruction continually in ways that support and extend learning.

FIGURE 6.1

In addition, the ways in which students participate in mathematics and express their mathematical identities determine their level of agency. Agency refers to the expression of one's identity (Murrell 2007). In mathematics classrooms, agency is how students take risks to make their mathematical thinking visible. A high sense of agency allows and encourages students to continue with the study of mathematics. Mathematical agency is about participating in mathematics in ways that are meaningful, both personally and socially (Berry 2016). Equitable mathematics teaching practices support identity and agency by creating structures for having students' mathematical ideas considered during instruction, supporting students in viewing themselves as having ownership of mathematical meaning, and coordinating enterprises across contexts to strengthen this ownership (Aguirre, Mayfield-Ingram, and Martin 2013; Oppland-Cordell and Martin 2015).

The importance of identity and agency cannot be understated; however, deficit views of students persist when students are labeled as "low" or "basic skills" or when a group of students is described as the "lowest I have ever seen." We must challenge this deficit narrative about our students' competence and attend to their beliefs about what mathematics is, what it means to be mathematically smart, and who can be smart in mathematics. Creating an authentic need for students to communicate and interact might be one of the most powerful practices we use to address deficit mindsets. Research has found that when students genuinely need one another and are encouraged to stick together through a difficult learning experience, they learn to notice and value the strengths each brings to the process (Jilk 2014). As a result, efforts to change how individual students think about themselves become a collective movement that perpetuates a classroom culture in which everyone celebrates: "We are all capable. We are all smart!" In this classroom culture, the empowerment of both teachers and students drives what we do and how we do it.

To address the need to focus on agency and identity, NCTM's *Catalyzing Change in High School Mathematics* (2018, 32–34) provides a crosswalk, shown in Figure 6.2, between the eight mathematics teaching practices in *Principles to Actions* (NCTM 2014) and equitable teaching practices.

As we discuss in greater detail in Chapter 10, on implementation, high school mathematics departments need to collaboratively discuss, work on implementing, exemplify, and share approaches to these practices via collegial classroom visits and video analyses of one another's teaching. In other words, as curriculum changes are implemented, converting all these words into tangible classroom practice is a nonnegotiable component of invigorating high school mathematics.

MATHEMATICS TEACHING PRACTICES: SUPPORTING EQUITABLE MATHEMATICS TEACHING

MATHEMATICS TEACHING PRACTICES	EQUITABLE TEACHING PRACTICES
Establish mathematics goals to focus learning. Effective teaching of mathematics establishes clear goals for the mathematics that students are learning, situates goals within learning progressions, and uses the goals to guide instructional decisions.	▪ Establish learning progressions that build students' mathematical understanding, increase their confidence, and support their mathematical identities as doers of mathematics. ▪ Establish high expectations to ensure that each and every student has the opportunity to meet the mathematical goals. ▪ Establish classroom norms for participation that position each and every student as a competent mathematics thinker. ▪ Establish classroom environments that promote learning mathematics as just, equitable, and inclusive.
Implement tasks that promote reasoning and problem solving. Effective teaching of mathematics engages students in solving and discussing tasks that promote mathematical reasoning and problem solving and allow multiple entry points and varied solution strategies.	▪ Engage students in tasks that provide multiple pathways for success and that require reasoning, problem solving, and modeling, thus enhancing each student's mathematical identity and sense of agency. ▪ Engage students in tasks that are culturally relevant. ▪ Engage students in tasks that allow them to draw on their funds of knowledge (i.e., the resources that students bring to the classroom, including their home, cultural, and language experiences).
Use and connect mathematical representations. Effective teaching of mathematics engages students in making connections among mathematical representations to deepen understanding of mathematics concepts and procedures and to use as tools for problem solving.	▪ Use multiple representations so that students draw on multiple resources of knowledge to position them as competent. ▪ Use multiple representations to draw on knowledge and experiences related to the resources that students bring to mathematics (culture, contexts, and experiences). ▪ Use multiple representations to promote the creation and discussion of unique mathematical representations to position students as mathematically competent.

FIGURE 6.2

MATHEMATICS TEACHING PRACTICES: SUPPORTING EQUITABLE MATHEMATICS TEACHING, *cont.*

MATHEMATICS TEACHING PRACTICES	EQUITABLE TEACHING PRACTICES
Facilitate meaningful mathematical discourse. Effective teaching of mathematics facilitates discourse among students to build shared understanding of mathematical ideas by analyzing and comparing student approaches and arguments.	▪ Use discourse to elicit students' ideas and strategies and create space for students to interact with peers to value multiple contributions and diminish hierarchal status among students (i.e., perceptions of differences in smartness and ability to participate). ▪ Use discourse to attend to ways in which students position one another as capable or not capable of doing mathematics. ▪ Make discourse an expected and natural part of mathematical thinking and reasoning, providing students with the space and confidence to ask questions that enhance their own mathematical learning. ▪ Use discourse as a means to disrupt structures and language that marginalize students.
Pose purposeful questions. Effective teaching of mathematics uses purposeful questions to assess and advance students' reasoning and sense making about important mathematical ideas and relationships.	▪ Pose purposeful questions and then listen to and understand students' thinking to signal to students that their thinking is valued and makes sense. ▪ Pose purposeful questions to assign competence to students. Verbally mark students' ideas as interesting or identify an important aspect of students' strategies to position them as competent. ▪ Be mindful of the fact that the questions that a teacher asks a student and how the teacher follows up on the student's response can support the student's development of a positive mathematical identity and sense of agency as a thinker and doer of mathematics.
Build procedural fluency from conceptual understanding. Effective teaching of mathematics builds fluency with procedures on a foundation of conceptual understanding so that students, over time, become skillful in using procedures flexibly as they solve contextual and mathematical problems.	▪ Connect conceptual understanding with procedural fluency to help students make sense of the mathematics and develop a positive disposition toward mathematics. ▪ Connect conceptual understanding with procedural fluency to reduce mathematical anxiety and position students as mathematical knowers and doers. ▪ Connect conceptual understanding with procedural fluency to provide students with a wider range of options for entering a task and building mathematical meaning.

FIGURE 6.2, *continued*   *continues*

MATHEMATICS TEACHING PRACTICES: SUPPORTING EQUITABLE MATHEMATICS TEACHING, *cont.*

MATHEMATICS TEACHING PRACTICES	EQUITABLE TEACHING PRACTICES
Support productive struggle in learning mathematics. Effective teaching of mathematics consistently provides students, individually and collectively, with opportunities and supports to engage in productive struggle as they grapple with mathematical ideas and relationships.	• Allow time for students to engage with mathematical ideas to support perseverance and identity development. • Hold high expectations, while offering just enough support and scaffolding to facilitate student progress on challenging work, to communicate caring and confidence in students.
Elicit and use evidence of student thinking. Effective teaching of mathematics uses evidence of student thinking to assess progress toward mathematical understanding and to adjust instruction continually in ways that support and extend learning.	• Elicit student thinking and make use of it during a lesson to send positive messages about students' mathematical identities. • Make student thinking public, and then choose to elevate a student to a more prominent position in the discussion by identifying his or her idea as worth exploring, to cultivate a positive mathematical identity. • Promote a classroom culture in which mistakes and errors are viewed as important reasoning opportunities, to encourage a wider range of students to engage in mathematical discussions with their peers and the teacher.

FIGURE 6.2, *continued*

The Time Principle and Brain Research

We have briefly summarized, in Chapter 3, how we urge teachers to launch sixty-minute lessons with warm-up activities like number talks (www.sfusdmath.org/math-talks -resources.html), reasoning exercises like Which One Doesn't Belong? (http://wodb.ca), and/or cumulative review. We hope that going over homework is never a time-wasting fifteen- to twenty-minute ordeal, but instead a brief period in which teachers post the answers to the homework exercises or problems on the whiteboard and provide students with five minutes to review their work in pairs or triads, with particular attention to the most troublesome problems. Technology should also be leveraged for students to submit their answers and for the teacher, using an item analysis, to intervene on the most difficult items. With respect to brain research on time on task in daily instruction, Eric Jensen (2005) provides educators with some important findings, such as:

- Newly processed information should be given immediate feedback (every ten minutes) for correction to occur before the information gets too fixed. Because the working memory is constantly grabbing from the hippocampus, review should occur within twenty-four hours, and again after seven days, or the hippocampus drops the information.

- Research shows that the brain becomes smarter (grows new dendrites) through trial and error because it enables the student to learn from experience how to eliminate poor choices. The brain-compatible teacher realizes the student rarely gets the right answer the first time after being exposed to new information and that nonthreatening activities like games and pair work provide a safe environment where the important stage of mistake making can occur.

Guidelines for direct instruction for various age groups are shown in Figure 6.3. Certainly, our virtual learning experiences during the pandemic make these guidelines clearer and more important than ever.

GRADE LEVEL	APPROPRIATE AMOUNT OF TIME FOR DIRECT INSTRUCTION
K–2	5–8 minutes
3–5	8–12 minutes
6–8	12–15 minutes
9–12	12–15 minutes
Adult learners	15–18 minutes

Source: Jensen (2005, 37)

FIGURE 6.3

Elements of Quality

Given these guidelines for equitable instruction, mathematics lessons must include the elements of quality instruction shown in Figure 6.4, which might serve as a short crib sheet for what should be done and what should be severely minimized as we plan, conduct, and reflect on mathematics instruction.

ELEMENTS OF QUALITY INSTRUCTION

EFFECTIVE PRACTICE	AS OPPOSED TO
Providing a clear statement and brief discussion of lesson goals	Saying merely "Lesson 4.5" or "pages 214–217"
Using engaging, relevant contexts	Using merely naked exercises
Using rich tasks and discussing their solutions	Using worksheets of exercises and focusing on just answers
Posing focused intentional oral and written questions	Just punting to stimulate thinking and discourse
Providing frequent opportunities for, and conveying expectations of, student discourse	Just telling and showing
Gradually revealing tasks, problems, data, and solutions	Just dumping large amounts of information and data
Consistently using multiple representations	Presenting just one way
Consistently seeking and presenting alternative approaches	Presenting just one way
Conveying clear expectations for explanations and justifications	Expecting just answers
Valuing and addressing common errors and misconceptions	Just focusing on right answers
Conveying consistent expectations that the mathematics should make sense as students construct understanding	Just lecturing with little regard to sense making
Gathering and using evidence of learning or the lack thereof	Just presenting material and letting the chips fall where they may

FIGURE 6.4

Examples

Here are three examples of how engaging tasks used with equitable teaching practices contribute mightily to invigorating mathematics.

EXAMPLE 1. An important theorem in calculus is the intermediate value theorem (IVT), which states that if a continuous function $f(x)$ on the interval $[a,b]$ has values of opposite sign inside an interval, then there must be some value $x = c$ on the interval (a,b) for which $f(c) = 0$. In traditional pedagogical approaches, the teacher provides the theorem verbatim and several examples of its use. In contrast, in the pedagogical approach used here, the teacher gradually reveals the task, focuses on student discourse, values common errors (see step 3), and allows students to construct deep understandings of the IVT.

> **Step 1** The images in Figure 6.5 are shown to students to foster a discussion of the definition of a root and allow them to arrive at their own understanding of what a root of a function is. (Note that the definition of a root is not provided by the teacher and not copied by the student.)

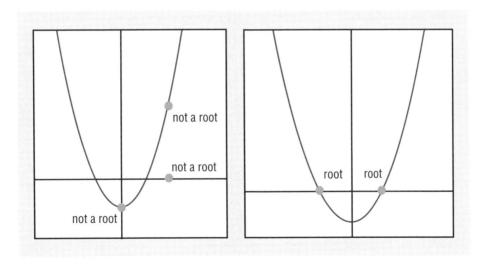

FIGURE 6.5

> **Step 2** Students are shown a function in the image in Figure 6.6a and asked if under each of the circles A, B, and C, there must be a root, there might be a root, or there cannot be a root. Extensive discourse occurs and then the image in Figure 6.6b is shown, revealing no root under A, a root under B, and no root under C. Students begin to develop the conditions necessary for a root to be present.

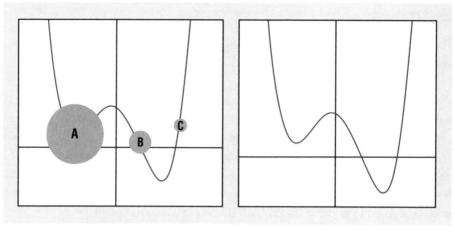

FIGURE 6.6A   **FIGURE 6.6B**

Step 3 Students are shown a new function (Figure 6.7a), again with three circles covering possible roots. They are once again asked if there must be a root, there might be a root, or there must not be a root. The reveal (Figure 6.7b) shows no root under A, no root under B, and to almost all students' surprise, no root under C. The discourse with respect to circle C is extensive and leads to the understanding that the function must be continuous on an interval for a root to occur on that given interval.

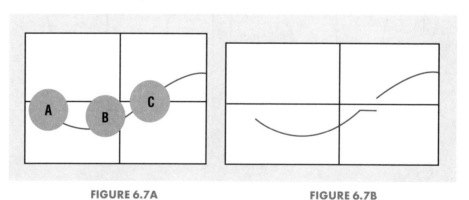

FIGURE 6.7A   **FIGURE 6.7B**

The full IVT lesson by Desmos is available at https://teacher.desmos.com /activitybuilder/custom/5c008dc00738f940aa109225.

Note how exactly the same important content can be taught in two very different ways with, very likely, two very different learning and understanding outcomes. Note, too, how the selection of tasks, the opportunity to explore, the power of technology to facilitate instantaneous feedback and provoke intense discussion, and the specific questions asked all contribute to a far more powerful lesson.

EXAMPLE 2. What do you notice? What do you wonder? The use of examples and non-examples leads to engaging opportunities for, and expectations of, student discourse about mathematics while students make sense, construct understanding, and notice/wonder. Figure 6.8 shows polyhedrons in two sets—one labeled "examples" and one labeled "non-examples." Students are asked to discuss the characteristics of the examples and come up with an understanding or definition of the polyhedrons pictured in the examples.

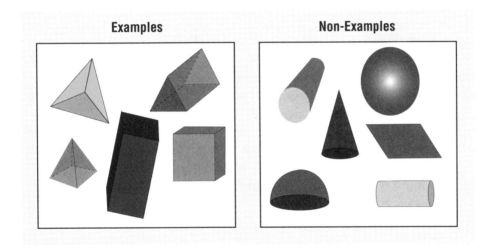

FIGURE 6.8

Note how the open-ended nature of "What do you notice?" and "What do you wonder?" provide access and opportunity for participation among all students. Note, too, how the lesson builds from student-generated ideas and questions, and thus promotes student ownership rather than teacher-directed pronouncement.

EXAMPLE 3. The use of context and rich tasks can lead students to make sense of mathematical content—formulas, procedures, or algorithms—through the context. This example (adapted from Hirsch and Fey 2008) starts with a contextual discussion about how many companies carry out market research to gather information about brand switching. The market research of three sneaker companies (Nike, Reebok, and Fila) is shown in Figure 6.9.

		NEXT BRAND		
		NIKE	REEBOK	FILA
CURRENT BRAND	NIKE	40%	40%	20%
	REEBOK	20%	50%	30%
	FILA	10%	20%	70%

FIGURE 6.9

Each entry in the table above is the percentage of customers who will buy a certain brand of shoe, given the brand they currently own. For example, the 30% in the second row and third column means that we can estimate that 30% of the people who now own Reebok will buy Fila as their next pair of shoes. Companies can use this information to make estimates of their future sales.

> **Assume that buyers purchase a new pair of shoes every year, and suppose this year 50 people bought Nike, 30 bought Reebok, and 20 bought Fila. How many people will buy each brand next year?**

Starting with the 50 people who bought Nike, most students can immediately determine that $50 \cdot 40\% = 20$ will buy Nike again. In addition, of the 30 who bought Reebok, $30 \cdot .2 = 6$ will switch to Nike, and of the 20 who bought Fila, $20 \cdot .1 = 2$ will switch to Nike, resulting in $20 + 6 + 2 = 28$ buyers of Nike in year two.

Many students will note that they used the percentages in the first column of the table above and multiplied each by the number of original buyers of each brand and then summed the results. Students are beginning to develop the understanding of how to multiply two matrices via the context of the problem.

Here again, the mathematics emerges from the context and from wrestling with data—giving students a greater reason to care—rather than the typical approach of abstractly presenting the formal mathematics long before ever applying it and seeing why it might actually be valuable to learn. In other words, this is another example of invigorating what we do through how we do it.

Observation and Collaboration

A teacher who doesn't collaborate works on an isolated island. When this lack of collaboration permeates an entire school, teachers more closely resemble independent contractors than colleagues. This lack of openness harms everyone. As we will discuss in greater depth in Chapter 10, observing colleagues in action is an important part of improving classroom instruction and implementing change. We must acknowledge that one of the best ways to improve instructional practice is to have colleagues observe one another and provide suggestions for improvements. We should welcome our colleagues' constructive feedback and practice giving it as well. Robert Kaplinsky started #ObserveMe to encourage teachers to observe each other and provide constructive feedback. Figure 6.10 shows one example.

Welcome! Please come inside and observe me. I'd love feedback on these goals:

- My students are engaged in their work.
- My students can describe what they are working on.
- My students are collaborating and/or helping each other.

#ObserveMe

FIGURE 6.10

Conclusion

There is little disagreement among all the major mathematics professional organizations that we need to move away from the use of traditional lecture as the sole instructional delivery method. Even within the traditional lecture setting, we should seek to more actively engage students than we have in the past. All mathematics organizations have stressed the importance of moving toward environments that incorporate multiple pedagogical approaches throughout the classroom, such as active learning models in which students engage in activities; problem solving that promote analysis, synthesis, and evaluation of class content; and cooperative learning that actively engage students in the learning process. We must promote such collaboration, provide opportunities to practice communicating ideas, and build agency and identity in students.

Guiding Questions

1. Among the mathematics teaching practices and the equitable teaching practices presented in Figure 6.2, which are currently commonly found in the majority of your school's mathematics classrooms? Why do you think this is?

2. Among the mathematics teaching practices and the equitable teaching practices presented in Figure 6.2, which are currently rarely found in the majority of your school's mathematics classrooms? Why do you think this is?

3. Reviewing the summary of effective practices found in Figure 6.4, which practices do you think would be appropriate places to start a process of shifting pedagogy?

7

The primary purpose of assessment is to inform and improve the teaching and learning of mathematics.

ELHAM KAZEMI, LYNSEY K. GIBBONS, KENDRA LOMAX,
AND MEGAN L. FRANKE (2016, 189)

Assessment

High-Quality Assessments That Hold Everyone Accountable

MANY EDUCATORS BELIEVE that assessment is the glue that holds the various components of education together. We know how essential it is that our assessments are closely aligned with our curriculum and our instruction. We know that what and how we assess is the best window on what we value. And we know that too often, when it comes to curriculum, instruction, and assessment—the three legs of our educational stool—the content, quality, and use of our assessments tend to get the least attention.

That is why our Chapter 3 guiding principle relating to assessment stated:

GUIDING PRINCIPLE

The high school mathematics program must recognize assessment as an integral part of instruction. At its core, what we assess and how we assess it communicate most clearly what we value. Accordingly, assessments must include a balanced portfolio of strategically aligned, common, and high-quality summative unit assessments and an array of quizzes and benchmark tasks and other formative assessment techniques.

NCTM's *Principles to Actions* (2014, 89) describes assessment this way: "Assessment provides evidence of proficiency with important mathematics content and practices, includes a variety of strategies and data sources, and informs feedback to students, instructional decisions, and program improvement."

However, for too many years, assessment has often been primarily seen as a vehicle for finding out what students have learned and has been used to determine grades. Educators have been inundated with different forms of assessment, such as quizzes, unit tests, standardized tests, projects, and portfolios. Moreover, it is very clear that too much weight is placed on results from large-scale, high-stakes assessments, which should never be used for diagnostic purposes. In fact, just the word *assessment* can be confusing, as it can be used in so many forms. Figure 7.1 provides a visual of the many forms of assessment separated into the two major types: summative and formative.

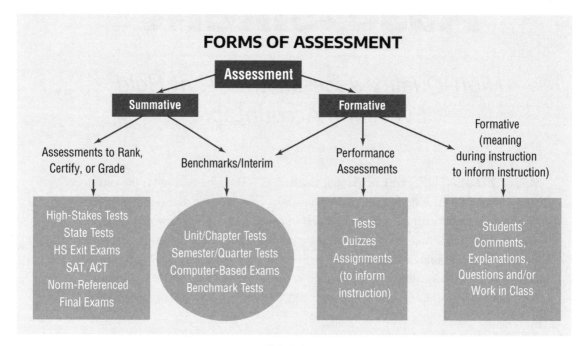

FIGURE 7.1

Principles to Actions (NCTM 2014) summarizes this variety of forms of assessment by noting that classroom mathematics assessment should serve four distinct functions in schools:

- monitoring students' progress to promote student learning
- making instructional decisions to modify instruction to facilitate student learning
- evaluating students' achievement to summarize and report students' demonstrated understanding at a particular moment in time
- evaluating programs to make decisions about instructional programs. (89)

Dan Meyer (2015) argues that students' thinking on assessment (and in class) is often thought of as correct or incorrect, as pictured in Figure 7.2.

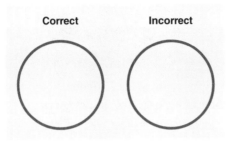

FIGURE 7.2

In fact, classroom reality is often closer to what is represented in Figure 7.3.

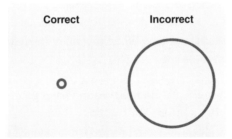

FIGURE 7.3

Mathematics teachers must change these perceptions about student learning and instead (as captured in Figure 7.4) attempt to understand what is interesting about students' learning on the basis of their responses to formative and summative assessment items. To simply score and grade on the basis of correct versus incorrect ignores the range of understandings revealed by correct work and accompanying explanations on the one hand and incorrect work that often reveals interesting insights and common misconceptions on the other.

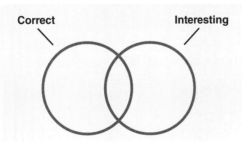

FIGURE 7.4

Given the importance of assessment, this chapter focuses on the benefits of formative assessment and the critical importance of common, high-quality unit assessments and innovative high-cognitive-demand assessment items.

Formative Assessment

In recent years, researchers have more closely examined the role assessment can play in actually enhancing student learning instead of just measuring it. This is now referred to as assessment for learning or formative assessment. Paul Black and his colleagues (2004) state:

> Assessment for learning is any assessment for which the first priority in its design and practice is to serve the purpose of promoting pupils' learning. It thus differs from assessment designed primarily to serve the purposes of accountability, or of ranking, or of certifying competence. An assessment activity can help learning if it provides information to be used as feedback, by teachers, and by their pupils, in assessing themselves and each other, to modify the teaching and learning activities in which they are engaged. (10)

John Hattie (2009) argues that no intervention has a greater effect than formative assessment done right. In addition, Wiliam and Thompson (2007) have found that formative assessment produces greater increases in students' achievement than class size or increases in teachers' content knowledge, and at a fraction of the cost. They propose that doing formative assessment right includes clarifying and sharing learning intentions and criteria for success in addition to conducting classroom discussions that elicit evidence of student understanding. Most importantly, formative assessment should provide feedback that moves learners forward prior to summative assessment. Lastly, it is imperative that teachers activate students as instructional resources for one another and activate students as owners of their own learning.

In other words, formative assessment is more diagnostic than evaluative. It is used to monitor students, to provide ongoing feedback; and to allow educators to improve and adjust their teaching methods. The information gathered is rarely marked or graded. Descriptive feedback may accompany formative assessment to let students know whether they have mastered an outcome or whether they require more practice.

Formative assessment examples include

- Impromptu quizzes.
- Anonymous polls.

- One-minute papers where students might write

    - the most surprising concept

    - questions not answered

    - the most confusing area of the topic

    - a question from the topic that might appear on the next test.

- Lesson exit tickets to summarize what pupils have learned. The website Read, Write, Think (readwritethink.org) has a plethora of exit slips, such as

    - The most important thing I learned today is . . .

    - I need help with . . .

    - I would like to learn about . . .

- A visualization or doodle map of what students have learned.

- My favorite "no." Students answer a question provided by their teacher and then analyze a wrong answer given by an anonymous classmate. The purpose of this activity is for the teacher to quickly assess how many students are grasping the concept and what in particular is causing any misunderstandings. For more details, see the video *My Favorite No (Uncut)* on the Teaching Channel website (https://learn.teachingchannel.com/video /my-favorite-no-complete-lesson).

- Two wrongs and a right. Which one is right and which two are wrong, and why?

Solve: $-2 - 3m < 5$ $-3m < 7$ $m > -\frac{7}{3}$	**Solve:** $-2 - 3m < 5$ $-3m < 7$ $m < 10$
Solve: $-2 - 3m < 5$ $-3m > 7$ $m < -\frac{7}{3}$	Two **wrongs** and a **right**

- 3-2-1 countdown:

    - 3 things you didn't know before

    - 2 things that surprised you about this topic

    - 1 thing you want to start doing with what you've learned.

Moreover, a multitude of technology apps (see Chapter 11) provide teachers with the opportunity to conduct formative assessment in diverse ways on a daily basis to provide daily feedback to our students and ourselves.

Common High-Quality Unit Assessment

We believe that one of the most important components of a high school mathematics program is a set of common, high-quality, balanced unit summative assessments toward which teachers in every course teach. We believe that these assessments should be common because it is unfair for students in two different classes of the same course to be held accountable on the basis of different instruments. We believe that high-quality assessments can only be constructed collaboratively and that students subjected to low-quality assessments are being unfairly penalized. And we believe that all such common unit assessments must be balanced in terms of skills, concepts, and applications and must be carefully aligned with unit standards and learning expectations.

Rather than ramble on about the characteristics of these common unit assessments, let's look at two examples that we believe have many positive characteristics and that are much stronger than many of the overwhelmingly skill-based, one-right-answer, high-memorization-load, low-depth-of-knowledge unit assessments we often encounter.

Figure 7.5 shows a sample Systems of Linear Equations unit test.

SYSTEMS OF LINEAR EQUATIONS UNIT ASSESSMENT

1. Is (4,–4) a solution of the system of linear equations? How do you know?

    $x - y = 8$

    $2x - y = 10$

2. Branch A of a company opened with 1 client and they get 5 new clients each week. Branch B opened with 10 clients and they get 2 new clients each week. A manager of the company wants to compare the number of clients, n, each branch has with respect to the number of weeks, w, since the company opened. Write a system of equations that the manager can use to compare the number of clients for each branch.

3. What is the most efficient method for solving the system of equations below? Explain why you choose the method and then use the method to solve the system.

    $t = w + 2$

    $2t + 3w = -26$

FIGURE 7.5

4. Write whole numbers in the boxes to create a system of linear equations that has no solution. Use only integers from 1 to 9.

   $y = 3(3x + 2)$

   $y = \square x + \square$

5. How many solutions will each system have?

$y = -2x$	$y = 4(2x - 1)$	$y = 3x + 2$
$y = 2x - 1$	$y = 8x - 4$	$y = 3x - 1$
$2x + 2y = 4$	$2x + 3y = 5$	$2x + 3y = 16$
$x + y = 2$	$4x + 5y = 20$	$3x + 4y = 17$

6. Create a system of linear equations with infinitely many solutions.

7. Create a system of linear equations with the solution (1,2).

8. Using the digits 1 to 9 at most one time each, fill in the boxes so that there are infinitely many solutions to the system of equations.

   $\square x + \square y = \square$

   $\square x + \square y = \square$

9. Graph the system of the equations and find the solution. Confirm your answer algebraically.

   $y = -2x + 1$

   $y = 2x - 1$

10. Draw a graph of a system of equations with no solution.

FIGURE 7.5, *continued*

Performance Assessment Take-Home Task

Using the integers from −9 to 9, at most one time each, create a system of three equations such that the solution is (1,1).

$y = \frac{\square}{\square} x + \square$

$y = \frac{\square}{\square} x + \square$

$y = \frac{\square}{\square} x + \square$

Source: Audrey Mendivil, Daniel Luevanos, and Robert Kaplinsky, from www.openmiddle.com

We believe that this is an exemplary unit assessment because

- The set of tasks appears to be closely aligned with any balanced set of learning expectations for this unit.
- It assumes that students can eventually use graphing tools to solve nearly all systems of equations, but that without conceptual understanding of how systems of linear equations work, they will be unable to complete applications that involve systems or interpret the solutions of these systems.
- It is limited to only ten tasks plus a do-at-home performance task with very little overlap in the requirements for successfully completing each task.
- Nearly all the tasks require some degree of thinking and reasoning, and all depend on conceptual understanding.
- There is a balance of Depth of Knowledge Level 2 and 3 tasks (see page 130 for a description of Depth of Knowledge), unlike the common emphasis on Depth of Knowledge Level 1 tasks.
- Many of the tasks have more than one right answer.

We encourage readers to compare this sample assessment with the unit test found for the corresponding chapter in most commonly used textbooks, as well as with the Systems of Linear Equations unit assessments used in your school.

Figure 7.6 shows a sample Volume and Surface Area unit test.

VOLUME AND SURFACE AREA UNIT ASSESSMENT

1. The volume of prism A is 48, and the volume of prism B is half the volume of prism A. What is the value of *a*?

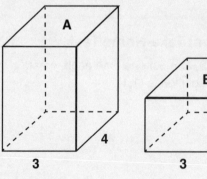
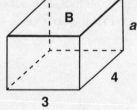

FIGURE 7.6

2. Write the volume of A in terms of B.

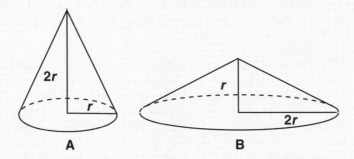

3. A plane intersects the center of a sphere with a volume of about 9,202.8 m³. What is the area of the cross section?

4. Create a cone with volume 120 in.³

5. Create a rectangular prism with surface area 48 in.²

6. What is the least and greatest amount of surface area possible for a rectangular prism with a volume of 64 in.³ and whole-number side lengths?

7. Using the digits 1 through 9, at most one time each, fill in the boxes to create two rectangular prisms so the volume of one rectangular prism is double the volume of the other.

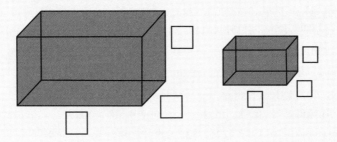

Source: Joe Schwartz

FIGURE 7.6, *continued*

Performance Assessment Take-Home Task

Build as *few* 3D shapes as possible to satisfy each constraint at least once. Include diagrams that make your thinking visual. Include all calculations.

A.	Has a diameter of 10cm	**B.**	Has a side length of 10cm
C.	Has a vertical height of 12cm	**D.**	Has a volume of 48cm³
E.	Has a slant height of 5cm	**F.**	Has a surface area of 360cm²
G.	Has a volume of 100 πcm³	**H.**	Has a slant height of 13cm

Which constraints pair nicely? Which constraints cannot be paired? Is it possible to solve in 2, 3, or 4 3D shapes? Describe how and why you built each 3D shape. Be sure to identify which 3D shapes satisfy which constraints.

Source: "3D Shapes Menu Math" created by Mary Bourassa and Nat Banting. Available at http://natbanting.com/menu-math.

We believe that these are exemplary unit assessments because

- Once again, there is a manageable, focused set of tasks that clearly answers the question "After four weeks of instruction on volume and surface area, exactly what do I want my students to know and demonstrate comprehension in to convince me and themselves that the important mathematics of this unit is understood?"
- Many of the tasks require students to "create" something.
- Again, rather than just asking students to parrot procedures or plug numbers into formulas, the tasks on this assessment ask students to demonstrate their understanding of the key ideas of volume and surface area.
- There is a balance of rather routine tasks and rather nonroutine tasks and a focus on Depth of Knowledge Levels 2 and 3 (see page 130).

Once again, readers are encouraged to compare this sample assessment with the unit test found for the corresponding chapter in most commonly used textbooks, as well as with the Volume and Surface Area unit assessments used in your school.

Assessment Items

Effective classroom assessment items provide evidence about students' mathematics learning. The evidence obtained depends on the questions and tasks used. More importantly, obtaining evidence about understanding and reasoning requires the use of deep items, tasks, and methods. Furthermore, as the use of technology has increased and students' expertise with technology has become ubiquitous, assessment items must change accordingly. Assessment items often are the same as they were fifty years ago, as seen in the 1970s seven-question Algebra 2 unit test in Figure 7.7.

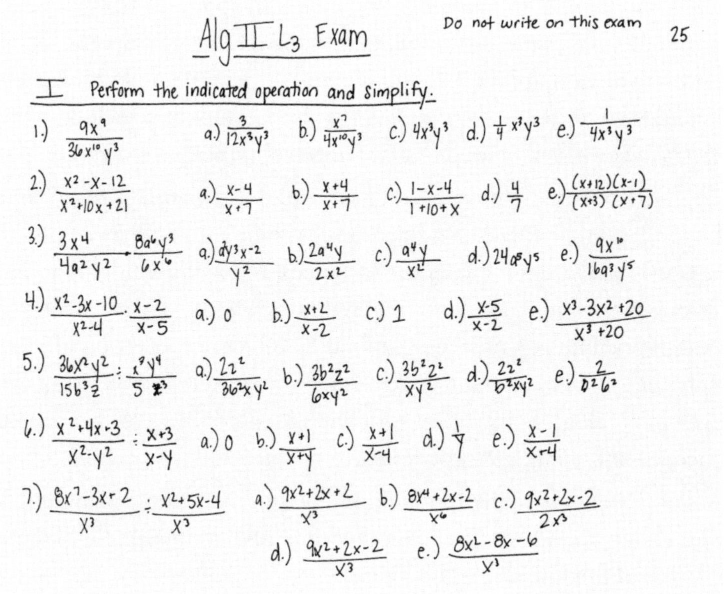

Alg II L_3 Exam — Do not write on this exam — 25

I Perform the indicated operation and simplify.

1.) $\frac{9x^9}{36x^{10}y^3}$ a.) $\frac{3}{12x^3y^3}$ b.) $\frac{x^7}{4x^{10}y^3}$ c.) $4x^3y^3$ d.) $\frac{1}{4}x^3y^3$ e.) $\frac{1}{4x^3y^3}$

2.) $\frac{x^2-x-12}{x^2+10x+21}$ a.) $\frac{x-4}{x+7}$ b.) $\frac{x+4}{x+7}$ c.) $\frac{1-x-4}{1+10+x}$ d.) $\frac{4}{7}$ e.) $\frac{(x+12)(x-1)}{(x+3)(x+7)}$

3.) $\frac{3x^4}{4a^2y^2} \cdot \frac{8a^6y^3}{6x^6}$ a.) $\frac{a^2y^3x^{-2}}{y^2}$ b.) $\frac{2a^4y}{2x^2}$ c.) $\frac{a^4y}{x^2}$ d.) $24a^8y^5$ e.) $\frac{9x^{10}}{16a^3y^5}$

4.) $\frac{x^2-3x-10}{x^2-4} \cdot \frac{x-2}{x-5}$ a.) 0 b.) $\frac{x+2}{x-2}$ c.) 1 d.) $\frac{x-5}{x-2}$ e.) $\frac{x^3-3x^2+20}{x^3+20}$

5.) $\frac{36x^2y^2}{15b^3z} \div \frac{x^3y^4}{5z^3}$ a.) $\frac{2z^2}{3b^2xy^2}$ b.) $\frac{3b^2z^2}{6xy^2}$ c.) $\frac{3b^2z^2}{xy^2}$ d.) $\frac{2z^2}{b^2xy^2}$ e.) $\frac{2}{b^2b^2}$

6.) $\frac{x^2+4x+3}{x^2-y^2} \div \frac{x+3}{x-y}$ a.) 0 b.) $\frac{x+1}{x+y}$ c.) $\frac{x+1}{x-4}$ d.) $\frac{1}{y}$ e.) $\frac{x-1}{x+4}$

7.) $\frac{8x^7-3x+2}{x^3} \div \frac{x^2+5x-4}{x^3}$ a.) $\frac{9x^2+2x+2}{x^3}$ b.) $\frac{8x^4+2x-2}{x^6}$ c.) $\frac{9x^2+2x-2}{2x^3}$ d.) $\frac{9x^2+2x-2}{x^3}$ e.) $\frac{8x^2-8x-6}{x^3}$

FIGURE 7.7

All the items on this assessment are skill based, fail to assess any conceptual understanding, lack application, and could easily be completed by students with the aid of Google, a CAS calculator, the Wolfram Alpha app, or a plethora of websites. Unfortunately, items like those in Figure 7.7 are still prevalent on many algebra exams today. While such procedural, low-level items should not be eliminated entirely on unit assessments, educators must diversify their items and include items that assess conceptual understanding and applications, items that increase cognitive demand, and innovative items that ask students to create, not just consume, mathematics.

A useful way to analyze items on any assessment is Webb's Depth of Knowledge (DoK) framework. DoK levels and descriptors can be used to guide item development and establish the cognitive demand for the assessment.

- Level 1 (Recall and Reproduction) includes recalling information such as a fact, definition, term, or simple procedure, as well as performing a simple algorithm or applying a formula. Key words include *identify*, *recall*, *recognize*, *use*, and *measure*. Verbs such as *describe* and *explain* could be classified at different levels depending on what is to be described and explained.

- Level 2 (Skills, Concepts, and Basic Reasoning) includes the engagement of some mental processing beyond a habitual response. A Level 2 assessment item requires students to make some decisions about how to approach the problem or activity, whereas Level 1 requires students to demonstrate a rote response, perform a well-known algorithm, follow a set procedure, or perform a clearly defined series of steps. Key words that generally distinguish a Level 2 item include *classify*, *organize*, *estimate*, *make observations*, *collect and display data*, and *compare data*.

- Level 3 (Strategic Thinking and Complex Reasoning) requires reasoning, planning, using evidence, and demonstrating a higher level of thinking than at the previous two levels. In most instances, requiring students to explain their thinking is at Level 3. Activities that require students to make conjectures are also at this level. The cognitive demands at Level 3 are complex and abstract. Level 3 activities include drawing conclusions from observations; citing evidence and developing a logical argument for concepts; explaining phenomena in terms of concepts; and using concepts to solve problems.

- Level 4 (Extended Thinking) requires complex reasoning, planning, developing, and thinking, most likely over an extended period of time. At Level 4, the cognitive demands of the task should be high and the work should be very complex. To be at this highest level, students are required to make several connections—relating ideas within the content area or among content areas—and to select one approach among many alternatives for how a problem should be solved. Level 4 activities include designing and conducting experiments; making connections between a finding and related concepts and phenomena; combining and synthesizing ideas into new concepts; and critiquing experimental designs.

The DoK progression examples in Figure 7.8 illustrate how mathematics assessment items can move students to deeper conceptual understanding. There are many resources available for DoK 2 and 3 items, including Robert Kaplinsky's Open Middle site at www.openmiddle.com.

DoK EXAMPLES

MATH CONTENT AREA	DOK 1: RECALL AND REPRODUCTION	DOK 2: SKILLS, CONCEPTS, AND BASIC REASONING	DOK 3: STRATEGIC THINKING AND COMPLEX REASONING
TWO-STEP EQUATIONS	**Solve** for x: $3x + 1 = 10$	**Create** two equations in the form $ax + b = c$ where a, b, and c are unique natural numbers between 1 and 9. In one equation, x should have a positive value, and in the other equation, x should have a negative value.	**Create** an equation in the form $ax + b = c$ where a, b, and c are unique natural numbers between 1 and 9 and where x has the **greatest** possible value.
EXPONENTS	**Evaluate** 2^6	**Create** three expressions in the form a^b that are equal to 64 and where a and b are unique natural numbers from 1 to 9 inclusive.	**Create** an expression in the form a^b with the largest three-digit answer where a and b and the digits in the answer are unique natural numbers from 1 to 9 inclusive.
GEOMETRY (AREA AND PERIMETER)	**Find** the perimeter of a rectangle with sides of 5 and 8.	**Create** at least four rectangles with a perimeter of 40.	**Create** a rectangle with a perimeter of 40 that has the greatest area.
SYSTEMS	**How many** solutions (0, 1, or infinite) does the system of equations have? $3x + 2y = 10$ $6x + 4y = 20$	**Create** a system of equations that has no solutions.	**Create** a system of equations that has the solution $(1, -2)$.
FACTORING	Factor $x^2 + 5x + 6$	**Create** a quadratic expression that is factorable by entering a number in the box. $2x^2 + 3x + \square =$	**Create** three trinomials using the digits 1 through 9 so that each can be written as a product of its rational factors. 1 2 3 4 5 6 7 8 9 $\square x^2 + \square x + \square$ $\square x^2 + \square x + \square$ $\square x^2 + \square x + \square$

FIGURE 7.8

It is clear that a deep conceptual understanding of mathematics is more important than ever in today's increasingly technological world. Moreover, such problems can challenge students at a competitive level. Another nontraditional assessment item measuring conceptual understanding is shown below.

Standard: Linear Equations

Item: Create a table with three points given the following constraints:

- The slope is positive.
- The *y*-intercept is negative.

As in the DoK 3 items in Figure 7.8, this item asks students to "create" and has multiple correct responses, such as

x	y	x	y	x	y
0	−2	−1	−3	1	1
1	−1	0	−1	2	5
2	1	1	1	3	9

All of which leads to the key question "What do these correct responses have in common?"

Nat Banting (http://natbanting.com/menu-math) expands upon this type of assessment item and provides students with a longer list of constraints that appear as an unordered list. Students must provide a mathematical object (equation, function, graph, etc.) to satisfy this list of constraints. Each constraint must be satisfied at least once, and students try to complete this goal using as few mathematical objects as possible. This preserves a low entry point (where teachers might ask students to design objects that satisfy one or two constraints), but escalates the possibility as students analyze which constraints pair well together and which cannot pair together.

Here are an algebra and a geometry task based on this idea:

Linear Functions Menu Task

Build as *few* linear functions as possible to satisfy each constraint at least once.

Record your functions in this form: $y = ax + b$

A.	Has a positive slope	B.	Has a positive y-intercept
C.	Has a negative x-intercept	D.	Never enters the first quadrant
E.	Goes through the point (1,−3)	F.	Has a slope of 0
G.	Has a negative slope	H.	Goes through the point (1,0)
I.	Never enters the second quadrant	J.	Has a slope between 0 and 1

This example with ten constraints provides an opportunity for students to productively struggle with many concepts at the same time and then decide which constraints pair nicely together, such as A and J. Students could also consider which constraints cannot be paired, such as A and G. Moreover, students need to determine how many functions are necessary to satisfy all ten constraints. Is it possible to solve in two, three, or four linear functions? Lastly, students should describe how and why they built each linear function and identify which linear functions satisfy which constraints.

Building Triangles Menu Task

Build as *few* triangles as possible to satisfy each constraint at least once. Any three distinct points can be joined to form a triangle. Build your triangles on a coordinate plane.

A.	Is an isosceles triangle	B.	Has a vertex in quadrant II
C.	Is a right triangle	D.	Has a vertex at (0,0)
E.	Has a side through (1,1)	F.	Is a scalene triangle
G.	Enters all four quadrants	H.	Has a 45° angle
I.	Has a vertex on the x-axis	J.	Is entirely in the first quadrant

Students should again decide which constraints pair nicely and which constraints cannot be paired. Is it possible to solve in two, three, or four triangles? Students should describe how and why they built each triangle and identify which triangles satisfy which constraints.

DoK Level 4 Performance Assessments

Level 4 tasks require complex reasoning, planning, developing, and thinking, most likely over an extended period of time. The cognitive demands of these tasks are high and the work is very complex. While DoK 4 tasks are not expected to be embedded in unit assessments, such tasks should still be part of a rich math curriculum. Here are some examples of such high-cognitive-demand performance tasks.

Task 1: Magic Squares

A three-by-three grid with the numbers 1 through 9 (used only one time each) is pictured below. The sum of each column, each row, and both diagonals is the same number (15). This configuration is called a magic square.

2	7	6
9	5	1
4	3	8

If we wanted to construct another magic square with different numbers but the same property that each column, each row, and both diagonals sum to the same number, it would take significant trial and error. Thus, instead we should examine the algebraic structure of the square. Let x be the center of the square and determine the expressions in terms of x (based on the original completed magic square) that would make up the remaining entries of the square.

$x - 3$	$x + 2$	$x + 1$
$x + 4$	x	$x - 4$
$x - 1$	$x - 2$	$x + 3$

The structure of the magic square has now been uncovered by algebra. Note that the sum of each column and each row is $3x$, and when $x = 5$, as in the first magic square, the sum is 15. Students can now create an infinite number of magic squares but *not* all the three-by-three magic squares. Why?

By furthering examining the structure of the magic square and using more algebra, students can determine the entire structure, as shown below. Note that the sum of each column, each row, and both diagonals is still $3x$. All three-by-three magic squares can now be constructed with this algebraic structure.

$x - y$	$x + y - z$	$x + z$
$x + y + z$	x	$x - y - z$
$x - z$	$x - y + z$	$x + y$

Task 2: Split 25 (from https://playwithyourmath.com)

Take the number 25 and break it up into as many addends as you wish (positive nonzero rational numbers only). What is the largest product you can make of those addends?

Addends	Sum	Product
10 + 10 + 5	25	500
5 + 5 + 5 + 5 + 5	25	3,125
2 + 2 + 2 + 2 + 2 + 2 + 2 + 2 + 2 + 2 + 2 + 2 + 1	25	4,096
2 + 2 + 2 + 2 + 2 + 2 + 2 + 2 + 2 + 2 + 2 + 3	25	6,144
3 + 3 + 3 + 3 + 3 + 3 + 3 + 3 + 1	25	6,561
3 + 3 + 3 + 3 + 3 + 3 + 3 + 4	25	8,748

The table above displays many attempts using natural numbers.
However, what about fractional values?

Addends	Sum	Product
2.5 + 2.5 + 2.5 + 2.5 + 2.5 + 2.5 + 2.5 + 2.5 + 2.5 + 2.5	25	9,536.7
$\frac{25}{9} + \frac{25}{9} + \frac{25}{9} + \frac{25}{9} + \frac{25}{9} + \frac{25}{9} + \frac{25}{9} + \frac{25}{9} + \frac{25}{9}$	25	9,846.4
$\frac{25}{8} + \frac{25}{8} + \frac{25}{8} + \frac{25}{8} + \frac{25}{8} + \frac{25}{8} + \frac{25}{8} + \frac{25}{8}$	25	9,094.9

A pattern seems to reveal itself, with the product increasing from $\left(\frac{25}{10}\right)$ to $\left(\frac{25}{9}\right)$ but then decreasing for $\left(\frac{25}{8}\right)$.

This structure implies quadratic behavior and thus the graph of $f(x) = \left(\frac{25}{x}\right)^x$ is shown in Figure 7.9.

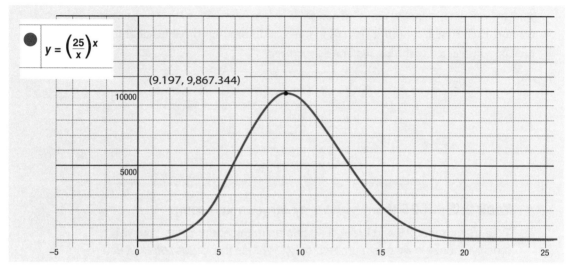

FIGURE 7.9

Why does the function reach a maximum at 9.197?

The mystery is solved when we realize that $\frac{25}{9.197} = e$ and thus the function reaches a maximum at $\left(\frac{25}{e}\right)^e = 9{,}867.3$.

Task 3: A Pythagorean Mystery (by James Tanton)

The numbers 1 through 10 inclusive are written on the board.

1	2	3	4	5
6	7	8	9	10

Choose two numbers, *a* and *b*, at random to use as the legs of a right triangle. Compute the hypotenuse, *h*. Place *h* on the board and erase *a* and *b*. Repeat this process eight more times until a single number remains. What is that number? Why?

Select 4 and 8. The hypotenuse with 4 and 8 as the legs of a right triangle is $\sqrt{80}$.

1	2	3		5	$\sqrt{80}$
6	7		9	10	

Select 1 and 2. The hypotenuse with 1 and 2 as the legs of a right triangle is $\sqrt{5}$.

		3		5	$\sqrt{80}$
6	7		9	10	$\sqrt{5}$

Select 3 and 5. The hypotenuse with 3 and 5 as the legs of a right triangle is $\sqrt{34}$.

		$\sqrt{34}$			$\sqrt{80}$
6	7		9	10	$\sqrt{5}$

Select 6 and 7. The hypotenuse with 6 and 7 as the legs of a right triangle is $\sqrt{85}$.

		$\sqrt{34}$			$\sqrt{80}$
	$\sqrt{85}$		9	10	$\sqrt{5}$

Select 9 and 10. The hypotenuse with 9 and 10 as the legs of a right triangle is $\sqrt{181}$.

		$\sqrt{34}$			$\sqrt{80}$
	$\sqrt{85}$			$\sqrt{181}$	$\sqrt{5}$

Select $\sqrt{85}$ and $\sqrt{34}$. The hypotenuse with $\sqrt{85}$ and $\sqrt{34}$ as the legs of a right triangle is $\sqrt{119}$.

					$\sqrt{80}$
	$\sqrt{119}$			$\sqrt{181}$	$\sqrt{5}$

Select $\sqrt{80}$ and $\sqrt{119}$. The hypotenuse with $\sqrt{80}$ and $\sqrt{119}$ as the legs of a right triangle is $\sqrt{199}$.

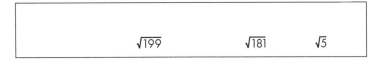

	$\sqrt{199}$		$\sqrt{181}$	$\sqrt{5}$

Select $\sqrt{199}$ and $\sqrt{5}$. The hypotenuse with $\sqrt{199}$ and $\sqrt{5}$ as the legs of a right triangle is $\sqrt{204}$.

Select $\sqrt{204}$ and $\sqrt{181}$. The hypotenuse with $\sqrt{204}$ and $\sqrt{181}$ as the legs of a right triangle is $\sqrt{385}$.

Why is the final answer $\sqrt{385}$?

Does it matter which numbers students select for a and b at the start?

These three high-cognitive-demand tasks challenge students with complex reasoning over a significant period of time. Other high-demand DoK 4 tasks can be found on the Math Assessment Project website at www.map.mathshell.org.

Conclusion

What appears on our classroom mathematics assessments tells students what we value about the mathematics that we teach. Thus, it is crucial that we assess the full range of mathematics, including conceptual understandings and high-cognitive-demand tasks, as illustrated in this chapter. Teachers, and school and district leaders, must

- make collaborative design and implementation of formative assessment processes a norm, and allocate the necessary time for same-course teams to complete this work
- make collaborative design and implementation of common unit assessments a norm, and allocate the necessary time for same-course teams to complete this work
- provide teachers with opportunities for professional development designed to develop assessment expertise
- ensure that collaborative teams use assessment results to guide and modify curricular tweaking, instructional practices, and program improvements.

Guiding Questions

1. What insights about assessment did you acquire as a result of reading this chapter?

2. What types of assessment are most and least commonly found in your classroom or the classrooms with which you are most familiar?

3. How would you compare the two sample unit assessments in this chapter with the typical unit assessments you currently use?

8

> Good technology extends and enhances [students']
> mathematical abilities, potentially offering
> a more level playing field for all.
>
> —STEPHEN ARNOLD

Technology

The Enabling Game Changer

WE ARE ALL AWARE that today's high school students were born into a world filled with technology, and, not surprisingly, using technology during mathematics instruction should be completely natural for them. After all, they are nearly all totally comfortable using technology to support their work in English language arts and social studies. It follows that the high school mathematics curriculum must make full use of technological tools that can engage students in the learning of mathematics and these tools must be ubiquitous throughout the curriculum, instruction, and assessment. We should subscribe to the belief that, as is the case throughout the worlds of commerce, medicine, science, and entertainment, the strategic use of technological tools is a critical component of increasing the productivity of instruction and the depth of learning.

It seems absurd to have to state these introductory thoughts in early 2021, but we often hear statements and questions like the following made with great confidence:

- "We don't allow our students to use graphing calculators in Algebra 1."
- "Why would we use Desmos when the SAT, ACT, and AP don't allow our students to use it?"
- "Letting my students use high-powered technology on tests is providing an open invitation for them to cheat."
- "If I let my students use technology all the time, I'd have to throw out a large part of the curriculum."

Our response to these not uncommon convictions is that without far greater reliance on technological tools, high school mathematics cannot be invigorated. Too many of our students fully understand—because computers, calculators, and Alexa do an amazing amount of mathematics homework in this country—that the world has changed and that readily available technology has empowered people while school mathematics has remained stagnant.

NCTM's position statement on technology is clear:

> It is essential that teachers and students have regular access to technologies—including classroom hardware, handheld and lab-based devices with mathematical software and applications, and Web-based resources—that support and advance mathematical sense making, reasoning, problem solving, and communication. Effective teachers optimize the potential of technology to develop students' understanding, stimulate their interest, and increase their proficiency in mathematics. When teachers use technology strategically, they can provide greater access to mathematics for all students. (NCTM 2015)

It is important to recognize that technology is driving changes that must be reflected in the mathematics curriculum and students' engagement with the content. Digital technology can serve three main functions (Drijvers, Boon, and Van Reeuwijk 2011):

1. as a tool for doing mathematics (e.g., when the purpose of a task is not to develop computational or symbolic manipulation expertise)

2. as a learning environment for fostering the development of conceptual understanding (e.g., illustrating the connection between functions and their graphs in a dynamic environment)

3. as a learning environment for practicing skills.

Similarly, the *2015 CUPM Curriculum Guide to Majors in the Mathematical Sciences* (MAA 2015) identifies five broad areas in which technology can be used to enhance teaching and learning: exploration, computation, assessment, communication, and motivation. Each of these will be expanded upon with examples.

Exploration

A plethora of sites, apps, and software (Desmos, Gizmos, GeoGebra, and others) allow students to use technology to explore concepts in mathematics classrooms. The goal of exploration is for students to engage with examples, deepen understanding, notice patterns, and make conjectures, and then transition to exploring proofs of correct conjectures. Exploration should culminate in statements of what has been discovered. Teachers must follow up and be sure students understand the mathematics that the exploration has illustrated.

The example in Figure 8.1, using the Desmos calculator, displays a quadratic function in vertex form with three dynamic sliders (*a*, *h*, and *k*). Students can move the sliders interactively and note the transformations of the function *f(x)*. The exploration should lead students to realize how each of these sliders transforms the function.

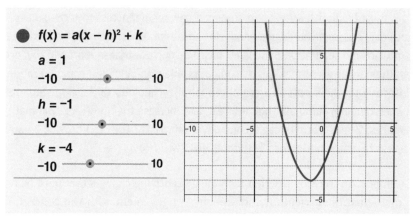

FIGURE 8.1

When students enter Calculus, the same graph can be presented, but this time *g(x)*, the derivative of *f(x)*, is graphed and now students determine the impact of *a*, *h*, and *k* on the derivative (see Figure 8.2). Can students anticipate that only *a* and *h* transform the derivative and *k* has no impact on it? Can students justify why or why not?

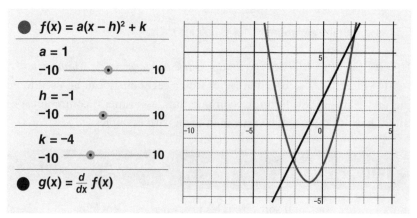

FIGURE 8.2

Next, *m(x)*, the second derivative of *f(x)*, can be graphed and similar questions can be asked (see Figure 8.3). Why is the second derivative a horizontal line? Which is the only slider that will transform the second derivative? Can students explain why?

This can be dynamically explored on the Desmos website (see www.desmos.com /calculator/2kowgi5qly).

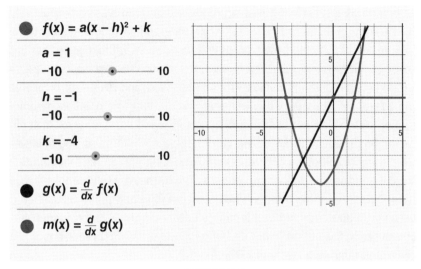

FIGURE 8.3

Computation

Technology can enable students to work with rich examples, realistic applications, and large data sets. In courses at all levels, substantial and realistic applications involve "messy" mathematics that makes calculating by hand difficult and unnecessary. Using technology opens the door for students to determine solution strategies, justify their analyses, and interpret the results. Authentic data and real situations should be used for developing mathematics concepts.

The advent of apps like Photomath, which students can use to obtain step-by-step solutions to simple arithmetic and algebraic expressions and equations, has angered many mathematics teachers. Why? Is it because now the inauthentic, traditional, symbolic manipulation can be done with technology? Similar equation apps and websites (e.g., Wolfram Alpha) are widely available on the web. And, of course, many handheld calculators with CAS capabilities can solve more complex problems than Photomath can. Such tools have ignited debates in mathematics education for decades, dating back to the invention of the first handheld, inexpensive, four-function calculator in the 1970s. The controversy stems from the concern that students will use the technology to cheat because the tools do the problem and often provide a step-by-step solution. We argue, however, that if using tools to solve problems is cheating, then we need to reconceptualize what cheating really is and what the purpose of mathematics skills is. Corey Webel and Samuel Otten (2015) argue:

> Computers are great at following instructions, and they can even learn inductively, by trying lots of things and "learning" what works and what does not. But so far they do not have intuition; they cannot draw conclusions without going back to a set of specific and literal rules. This is why the most sophisticated robots have such a hard time recognizing commonplace objects (Strickland 2013), which children can do well before they are two years old. It is also why PhotoMath sometimes cannot tell the difference between the variable x and the symbol for multiplication. On the other hand, students can intuit ideas without resorting to logical rules. They can pick up subtle contextual cues, and they can see mathematical structure and use that in their thinking. This is why they can solve problems they have never seen before, whereas PhotoMath can solve only problems that it has been taught how to solve. What is more, students can also invent new problems by wondering and posing "what-ifs." Of course, they can do these things only if given opportunities to do them. (372)

In other words, we must distinguish between tasks for technology (e.g., calculating trig ratios) and tasks for students (e.g., understanding trig ratios). Conrad Wolfram (2010) argues emphatically that the part of math we teach—calculation by hand—is not just tedious but mostly irrelevant to real mathematics and the real world. It is clear that much of high school mathematics is asking students to spend too much time completing tasks better suited to technology tools and not enough time engaging in mathematics in ways for which their minds are especially well suited, such as searching for patterns, making conjectures, and critiquing reasoning.

Assessment (and Homework)

When using technology for assessment and/or homework, technology can inform both the teacher and the student of what needs improvement. Online homework/assessment systems with immediate feedback are becoming more widely used across the country. Examples include

- www.deltamath.com
- www.mathxlforschool.com
- www.edulastic.com
- www.mathtv.com

Such sites provide the benefits of automatically graded assignments, personalized and differentiated homework, and immediate feedback for students. Some digital homework systems incorporate tutorials that can support learners and provide information to teachers in real time during class. Tutorials range from traditional YouTube videos to Khan Academy to digitally enhanced tutorials with embedded assessment, such as https://edpuzzle.com. Technology also pushes assessment practices by challenging teachers to construct examination questions that cannot be entirely answered by technology (see Chapter 7, on assessment).

We argue that digital homework can increase students' interest in doing homework, easily allow students multiple tries, boost students' efficiency in submitting homework, and allow teachers to provide more immediate feedback. In addition, digital assessment feedback is often more than just right or wrong feedback. Technology can provide students with support for their thinking. For example, when students graph functions, technology can show them the implications of their thinking. Maybe the parabola needs to shift left, or open a bit more slowly, or open downward. Students can respond to the feedback and get more feedback on their next attempt.

Communication and Intrinsic Motivation

Christopher Danielson and Dan Meyer (2016) wrote about the principles that guide their lesson development work. These principles include using the technology to connect students to one another, supporting collaboration, and promoting discourse. Rather than being used for the purpose of connecting individual students to the teacher or to artificial intelligence, technology can be used to connect students with one another so that students can share ideas, ask questions of one another, and challenge one another in rich and interesting ways. When used in this way, technology facilitates showing students the solutions of their classmates, challenging students with new tasks their classmates have designed, and sharing comments and solutions for those shared tasks.

For example, Guess Who? is a childhood game in which one person chooses a character and the other person must ask yes-or-no questions to determine which character was chosen. This game can be "played" on the computer with mathematics functions, images, or numbers via the teacher.desmos.com platform. Students are shown an array of choices. One student secretly selects an object and the other student must ask yes-or-no questions that lead to identifying the selected object. The goal is for students to arrive at the correct object with the fewest number of questions. In this manner, students are communicating with each other through the technology, asking a set of questions, and using vocabulary to limit the available objects to a single one. Feedback is provided by the student's partner and can be monitored by the computer or the teacher. The sample in Figure 8.4 is designed to spark vocabulary-rich conversations about various functions. Key vocabulary that may appear in student questions includes *linear, quadratic, exponential, cubic, absolute value, rational, radical, sinusoid,* and *step.*

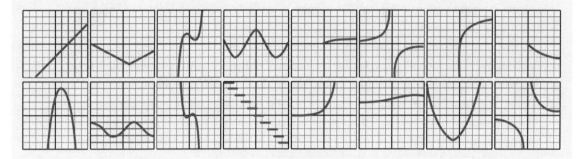

FIGURE 8.4

When students take ownership of their learning, they are motivated to persevere and succeed. Pedagogical strategies that incorporate technology can actively engage students in exploring and discovering ideas, solving problems, communicating their ideas to others, and reflecting on their own thinking. Effective motivation tends to be intrinsic—we do something because we want to do it.

Productive and Unproductive Beliefs About Technology

NCTM's *Principles to Actions* (2014, 82–83) compares sets of unproductive and productive beliefs that influence the implementation of classroom tools and technology (see Figure 8.5). We should not view these beliefs as good or bad; rather, we should understand that some beliefs are unproductive when they limit student access to important mathematics content and practices, while other beliefs support effective teaching and learning.

BELIEFS ABOUT TOOLS AND TECHNOLOGY IN LEARNING MATHEMATICS

UNPRODUCTIVE BELIEFS	PRODUCTIVE BELIEFS
Calculators and other tools are at best a frill or distraction, and at worst a crutch that keeps students from learning mathematics. Students should only use these tools after they have learned how to do the procedure with paper and pencil.	Technology is an inescapable fact of life in the world we live and should be embraced as a powerful tool for doing mathematics. Use of technology can assist students to visualize and understand important mathematical concepts and support students' mathematical reasoning and problem solving.
School mathematics is static. What students need to know about mathematics is unchanged (or maybe even threatened) by the presence of technology.	Technology and other tools not only change how to teach but also affect what can be taught. They can assist students in investigating mathematical ideas and problems that might otherwise be too difficult or time-consuming to explore.
Hands-on and virtual manipulatives should only be used with very young children who need visuals and opportunities to explore through moving objects.	Students at all grade levels can benefit from the use of hands-on and virtual manipulative materials to provide visual models of a range of mathematical ideas.
Technology should be primarily used as a quick way to get correct answers to computations.	Finding answers to a mathematical computation is not sufficient. Students need to understand if an answer is reasonable and how the results apply to a given context. They also need to be able to consider the relative usefulness of a range of tools in particular contexts.
Only select individuals, such as the most advanced students or students who reside in districts who choose technology as a budgetary priority, should have access to useful technology and tools since these are optional add-ons to mathematics learning.	All students should have access to technology and other tools that support the teaching and learning of mathematics.

FIGURE 8.5

continues

BELIEFS ABOUT TOOLS AND TECHNOLOGY IN LEARNING MATHEMATICS, *cont.*

UNPRODUCTIVE BELIEFS	PRODUCTIVE BELIEFS
Using technology and other tools to teach is easy. Just launch the app or website, or hand out the manipulatives, and let the students work on their own.	Effective use of technology and other tools requires careful planning. Teachers need appropriate professional development to learn how to use them effectively.
Online instructional videos can replace traditional classroom instruction.	Online instructional videos must be judiciously adopted and used to support, not replace, effective instruction.

FIGURE 8.5, *continued*

Conclusion

New technologies for mathematics instruction often make us feel uncomfortable. Nonetheless, we encourage mathematics teachers to see such tools not as threats, but rather as opportunities to clarify what is important in the learning and teaching of mathematics. Such technology (current and not yet invented) can be harnessed in mathematics classrooms to

- Shift the focus from learning many individual procedures for algebraic manipulations to considering multiple equivalent forms of expressions and equations, interpreting the results of manipulations, and making strategic choices about which forms of an expression or equation to use.
- Approximate solutions and use the context to reason about the degree of precision required. Equations that cannot be solved exactly by following a set of procedures known to the student can nonetheless be solved by reasoning about the numbers and the structure of the equation.
- Allow access to large data sets, organize and manage the data, take random samples, and test conjectures by resampling—all central elements in the world of big data.

- "Clean" and organize data, including very large data sets, into a useful and manageable structure—a first step in any analysis of data.

- Create simulations and serve as a powerful tool by enabling students to create a visual image of the key features of a sampling distribution for a sample statistic.

- Explore known properties of geometric figures and discover new properties, providing results that call for and demonstrate the power of deduction.

- Create dynamic geometry transformations that result in the discovery of properties and theorems.

We close with a thought-provoking idea from Conrad Wolfram (2020): In his utopian classroom, students would know when to use the quadratic equation, a basic algebra concept, and how to set it up. Then the computer would step in and do the calculation. Wolfram estimates that about 80 percent of most math curricula involves rote hand calculations—redundant exercises like long division and exponential functions. Why bother with that mess when a computer can calculate it in seconds and with much greater accuracy? That time could be spent becoming data literate.

Guiding Questions

1. What are some of the most effective uses of technology you have experienced, and why do you think they were so effective?

2. Reflecting on the examples embedded in this chapter, in what ways can technology support higher levels of learning?

3. Considering the unproductive beliefs listed in Figure 8.5, what strategies might be employed to shift colleagues from their unproductive beliefs to the more productive beliefs in the figure?

Modeling mathematics and statistics
should be key components throughout
any high school mathematics program.

—NCTM (2018, 41)

Modeling

The Overarching Twenty-First-Century Competency

IN CHAPTER 3, for the guiding principle for context and modeling, we noted:

> **GUIDING PRINCIPLE**
> *The high school mathematics program must include situations, applications, and contemporary problems, often interdisciplinary in nature, that illustrate the usefulness of mathematics and employ mathematical modeling. Relevant contexts include worthwhile mathematical tasks, interesting applications, real-world opportunities to employ mathematical modeling, and problem-based lessons that motivate learning.*

We have also frequently referred to modeling in the course descriptions in Chapters 4 and 5. But what exactly is this relatively new addition to high school math, and why is it so important to add to our coursework?

Mathematical modeling is central to, and essential for, providing high school students with opportunities to use their mathematical understanding to make greater sense of the world. A mathematical model is a representation of a particular real-world situation that attempts to describe, explore, and understand it. Modeling requires decision-making that involves determining which aspects of the phenomenon to include in the model, which to ignore, and what kind of mathematical representations to select. The mathematical modeling cycle begins with a real problem and involves a number of steps (NGA Center and CCSSO 2010; Bliss et al. 2016):

- formulating the problem or question
- stating assumptions (often requiring simplifications of the real situation) and defining variables
- restating the problem or question mathematically
- solving the problem using the mathematical model
- analyzing and assessing the solution
- refining the model, going back to the first steps if necessary
- reporting the results.

The first step is missing from almost all mathematics questions, textbooks, and lessons. Note that Albert Einstein, nearly a century ago, stated: "The formulation of the problem is often more essential than its solution, which may be merely a matter of mathematical or experimental skill" (Einstein and Infeld 1938, 92).

The *Guidelines for Assessment and Instruction in Mathematical Modeling Education* (*GAIMME*) provide teachers five guiding principles for mathematical modeling:

- Modeling is open-ended and messy.
- When students are modeling, they must be making genuine choices.
- Modeling problems can be developed from familiar tasks.
- Assessment should focus on the process and not on the product or pieces only.
- Modeling happens in teams. (*GAIMME: Guidelines for Assessment and Instruction in Mathematical Modeling Education*, Sol Garfunkel and Michelle Montgomery, editors, COMAP and SIAM, Philadelphia, 2016)

In high school algebra, the modeling cycle provides students an opportunity to deepen their understanding of the value of representing relationships between quantities by using symbolic notation, developing general rules for calculations, and connecting mathematical structures to their symbolic, graphic, and tabular representations. Comparing multiple models for the same scenario can lead to further opportunities to discuss what different symbolic representations reveal about the scenario and to experience the value of algebraic models. In geometry, experiencing the mathematical modeling cycle from the simplification of the real problem through the solving of the simplified problem, the interpretation of its solution, and the checking of the solution's feasibility, introduces geometric techniques, tools, and points of view that are valuable to problem solving.

Henry O. Pollak (2013), one of the pioneers in the teaching of mathematical modeling in schools, makes it clear that mathematical modeling is not just a new and pretentious name for "word problems" or "problem solving." The sole purpose of a word problem is to practice the mathematics of the current lesson. Moreover, problem solving rarely refers to the outside world at all. Even when it does, problem solving usually begins with the idealized real-world situation in mathematical terms, and ends with a mathematical result and a solution in the back of the book. Mathematical modeling, on the other hand, begins in the "unedited" real world, requires problem formulating before problem solving, and, once the problem is solved, moves back into the real world where the results are considered in their original context. A typical word problem and a modeling problem with respect to surface area are shown below for comparison.

> **Word Problem: A cylindrical cup is made out of plastic. It is 5 inches tall and has a radius of 1.75 inches. How many square inches of plastic sheeting were used to make the cup?**

> **Modeling Problem: Overheard in the ER as the sirens blare: "Oh my, look at this next one. He's completely burned from head to toe." "Not a problem, just order up 1,000 square inches of skin from the graft bank." Which response, "Oh good" or "Uh-oh," is more appropriate? Explain your thinking. Assuming you are the patient, how much skin would you hope they ordered up?**

Dan Meyer (2015) breaks down the pedagogical process of modeling into four different actions through which teachers should guide students when using modeling tasks (see Figure 9.1).

MODELING COMPONENT	STUDENT ACTIONS	QUESTIONS
1. Identifying essential variables in a situation	Students identify essential variables in a situation and decide what information matters for a given task and also what does not matter.	• What have you assumed in order to solve the problem? • Why did you make these choices? • What information is necessary, and what information is unnecessary?
2. Formulating models from those variables	Students formulate models from those variables using tables, graphs, and/or equations. Students both see the need for these models and understand them with teacher support. Students should experience how disorganized numbers become without a table to organize them or how opaque those numbers become without a graph to visualize them.	• Where did you find the numbers that you used in your model? • What pictures, diagrams, or graphs might help people understand your information, model, and results?
3. Performing operations using those models and interpreting the results of those operations	Students perform operations using their models and interpret the results of those operations. Students should recognize that the world will rarely fully validate the conclusions drawn from their models and that some uncertainty is to be expected. Students learn that mathematics is smooth and frictionless, whereas the world (and their models) is rough and full of surprises.	• How do you know you have a good and useful model? • Why does your model make sense? • What are the most important things for your audience to understand about your model and/or solution?
4. Validating the conclusions of those results	Students validate the conclusions by performing an internal error check and correcting or improving their models as needed. Sometimes they validate the models when they watch how well they predict.	• Does this make sense? • Have I forgotten anything?

FIGURE 9.1

Modeling Examples

Example 1: An Irrigation System

A linear irrigation system consists of a long water pipe set on wheels that keep it above the level of the plants. Nozzles are placed along the pipe, and each nozzle sprays water in a circular region. The entire system moves slowly down the field at a constant speed, watering the plants beneath as it moves. You have 300 feet of pipe and 6 nozzles available. The nozzles deliver a relatively uniform spray to a circular region 50 feet in radius. How far apart should the nozzles be placed to produce the most uniform distribution of water on a rectangular field 300-feet wide?

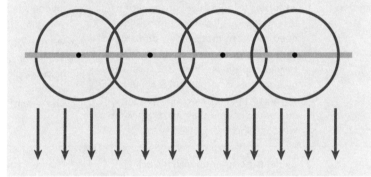

Source: GAIMME: Guidelines for Assessment and Instruction in Mathematical Modeling Education, *Sol Garfunkel and Michelle Montgomery, editors, COMAP and SIAM, Philadelphia, 2016*

FIGURE 9.2

In this problem, students must realize that the amount of water sprayed on a particular point in the field by a single nozzle is proportional to the length of the chord of that nozzle's circle passing over that point. The areas of the field watered by two sprinkler heads receive an amount of water proportional to the sums of the chord lengths. Students should recognize that they only need to consider the portion of the field between the two adjacent nozzles.

Students will need to find that the length of a chord x feet from the center of a nozzle is $2y = 2\sqrt{50^2 - x^2}$ and that if the nozzles are D feet apart, then the point that is x feet from one nozzle is also $D - x$ feet from the neighboring nozzle, allowing computation of the corresponding chord length in that watering circle.

Students might work in groups to compute the lengths of all the chords at 1-foot intervals between the two nozzles. Note that students should realize that there is no distance between nozzles that gives a completely uniform distribution of water across the field. Thus, they need to define some measure of uniformity of the distribution, perhaps motivated by examining the closest-together and farthest-apart extreme cases of nozzle placement.

Example 2: Starbucks Modeling Task

Starbucks has a huge number of stores in the United States. In many places, you can see two Starbucks down the block from each other. Rumor has it that there is even an intersection in Houston, Texas, with three Starbucks (can you find it?). However, in 1992 there were only 146 Starbucks locations in the entire United States. How many Starbucks do you think there were in the United States in 2020? Make a quick estimate.

The graph in Figure 9.3 shows the number of Starbucks locations in the United States at several points in time (1992–2008). (Students could also find such data on the internet.)

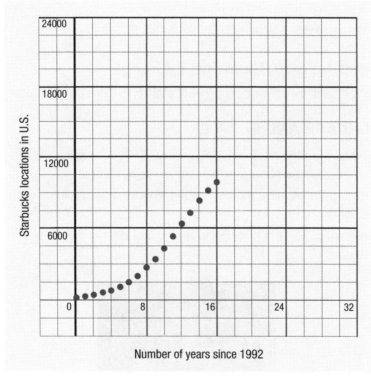

FIGURE 9.3

What mathematics function would be appropriate to model the relationship between the number of locations (*y*-axis) and the number of years since 1992 (*x*-axis)? Might it be exponential? Students can collect and graph additional data (after 2008). What model might be appropriate now? Might it be logistic? Why is the growth of Starbucks locations probably not exponential? In general, what kind of situations do you think will be better modeled by logistic functions (as compared to exponential)? One might also examine the pandemic data (infections over time). Why are those data logistic also?

This modeling lesson can be found in more detail on teacher.desmos at https://teacher.desmos.com/activitybuilder/custom/564d37a2895eb8280b0bfe0d.

Three-Act Tasks

A unique kind of mathematical modeling pedagogy called a three-act task was developed by Dan Meyer in 2010. A three-act task is a modeling task consisting of three distinct parts: an engaging and perplexing Act 1, an information- and solution-seeking Act 2, and a solution-discussing and solution-revealing Act 3. One main reason why these tasks are so successful in high school classrooms is that there is a low entry point and a high intrigue level. An outline of the methodology is presented below using two sample tasks.

Three-Act Lesson, Example 1: Charge
(by Michael Fenton, from http://reasonandwonder.com/charge)

ACT 1: ENGAGE AND PERPLEX

- The teacher shares with students an image, video, or other situation that is engaging and perplexing, such as the image in Figure 9.4.
- Students discuss what they notice and wonder. They generate questions to ask about the situation.
- Students decide on a question to answer and make estimates about the likely solution.

FIGURE 9.4

Students notice and wonder many intriguing things about the image, making comments such as those in Figure 9.5.

NOTICES	WONDERS
I noticed that the phone is at 5%.	I wonder when they started charging the phone.
I noticed that this person uses their phone a lot.	I wonder why they have Izcomm.
I noticed they have Izcomm.	I wonder what year this is.
I noticed that it is July 11 on Friday.	I wonder what kind of iPhone that person has.
I noticed that at 9:02 the battery was charging.	I wonder how long it will take to charge.
I noticed that the phone was on "do not disturb."	I wonder how long it will take to die.
I noticed that this person is probably punctual (they have an alarm set).	I wonder if it is 9:02 a.m. or p.m.

FIGURE 9.5

ACT 2: SEEK INFORMATION AND SOLUTIONS

- Students work on finding solutions to their problems.
- They use information they have from Act 1 and ask for more information. The teacher supplies more information, such as the images in Figure 9.6, only as it is requested by students.

FIGURE 9.6

Students select a representation such as a table and/or graph of the four data points provided (see Figure 9.7). Also, the line $y = 100$, which represents when the phone would be 100% charged, might be useful.

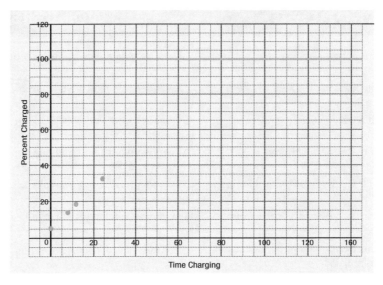

FIGURE 9.7

Computing slope and intercept from the data points and using a linear model $f(x) = 76x + 5$ yields a full charge after 81.429 minutes or about 1 hour and 21 minutes (see Figure 9.8).

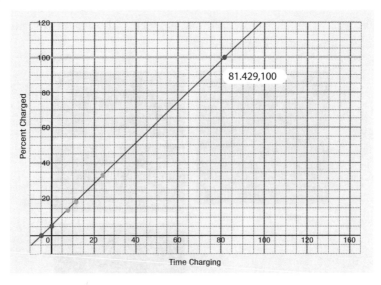

FIGURE 9.8

ACT 3: REVEAL, DISCUSS, EXTEND!

- Students share their work, their thinking, and their solutions.
- There is a reveal by the teacher of a student's solution, and a discussion ensues about the student's model.
- Students compare their solutions to their estimates and discuss their comparisons.
- Students discuss the assumptions that were made in their work.
- Students think of other questions about, extensions to, and proposed changes to their model.

The reveal for this activity shows a linear relationship for about 80% of the charge but then a nonlinear relationship for the remaining time of the charge, yielding a time of 140 minutes (2 hours and 20 minutes) when fully charged (see Figure 9.9). This leads to many interesting questions.

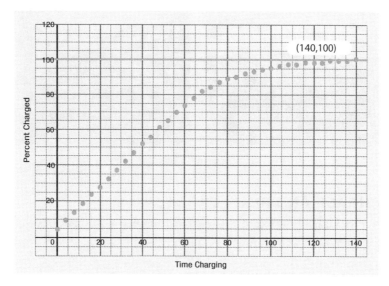

FIGURE 9.9

As an extension, students could collect their own data using their own phones and explore different variables, including what kind of charger was used, whether the phone was being used during charging, and what type of phone was being charged. Explore more at www.desmos.com/calculator/hzlch8fx0x.

Three-Act Lesson, Example 2: Toilet

(by Robert Kaplinsky, from https://robertkaplinsky.com/work/toilet/)

The teacher explains that one type of toilet comes in two models: dual flush or single flush (see Figure 9.10). The dual flush toilet has two buttons: one flushes "solids" with more water and "liquids" with less water. The single flush toilet always flushes with the same amount of water, which is an amount less than solids for the dual flush but more than liquids.

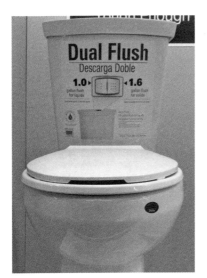

FIGURE 9.10

ACT 1: ENGAGE AND PERPLEX

Students consider if it is possible that after some number of flushes both toilets would use the same amount of water. Students explain how they know.

ACT 2: SEEK INFORMATION AND SOLUTIONS

The information that students need to know is the amount of water each toilet uses. The toilets use the unit gpf or gallons (of water used) per flush. The dual flush toilet uses 1.6 gpf for "solids" and 1.0 gpf for "liquids" while the single flush always uses 1.28 gpf.

Students investigate how many flushes, solid and liquid on the dual flush, versus how many flushes on the single flush would use the same number of gallons. 100 flushes on the single flush and 128 flushes on the liquids for the dual flush would both use 128 gallons. Students' task is to find the fewest number of flushes.

ACT 3: REVEAL, DISCUSS, EXTEND!

Student 1 response:

You know that the single flush toilet always uses 1.28 gpf. So, let's examine ratio of "liquids" to "solids" on the dual flush toilet that also gives an average of 1.28 gpf.

- If 1:1, then dual flush averages 1.3 gpf.
- If 2:1, then dual flush averages 1.2 gpf.
- If 8:7, then dual flush ratio is exactly 1.28 gpf.

Student 2 response:

$1.0 \cdot x + 1.6 \cdot y$ = total water usage for dual flush **and** $1.28 \cdot x + 1.28 \cdot y$ = total water usage for single flush. Where x is the number of "liquid" flushes and y is the number of "solid" flushes. Solving these two equations equal to each other yields $y = 0.875x$.

How are these student responses similar and how are they different? How is the equation $y = 0.875x$ reflected in the ratios in student 1's response?

As an extension, students could examine the prices of the toilets.

The Power of Modeling

Here is what we hope readers draw from these examples:

- Mathematical modeling tasks integrate, apply, and reinforce large chunks of important mathematical skills and concepts.
- Used effectively, mathematical modeling tasks can teach, not just review, key mathematical ideas.
- Mathematical tasks, whether algebraic, geometric, or statistical, enable the powerful pedagogical practices of justification, estimation, iteration, multiple representations, and alternative approaches—all key aspects of how mathematics is used outside school.
- Mathematical modeling tasks expect, and even demand, access to technological tools.
- Almost by definition, mathematical modeling tasks obviate the "Why are we doing this?" question because the purpose and value are evident.
- Mathematical modeling tasks are often interdisciplinary, linking mathematics to science, social studies, and/or the arts.

- Mathematical modeling tasks are powerful motivators of student interest.
- Generating the reports that emerge from mathematical modeling tasks provides essential preparation for college and the world of work.

In short, a perusal of these benefits should make it clear that the gradual replacement of piles of practice worksheets and dozens of exercises—often focusing on increasingly obsolete skills—with a few carefully selected mathematical modeling tasks is an accessible and effective strategy for invigorating high school mathematics.

Additional Tasks to Try

A plethora of modeling and three-act tasks are available on the internet. Figure 9.11 lists a few of our favorite ones from www.101qs.com. Search for title and author in the search engine on the website. Additional resources are provided in Chapter 11.

CONTENT	TASK	SEARCH TITLE	AUTHOR
VOLUME	How many cookie boxes fit in the SUV?	Girl Scout Cookies	Dan Meyer
PYTHAGOREAN THEOREM	Which path is fastest to the taco cart?	Taco Cart	Dan Meyer
QUADRATICS	Will the basketball score?	Will It Hit the Hoop?	Dan Meyer
SYSTEMS OF EQUATIONS	When are the stacks of cups equal?	Stacking Cups	Andrew Stadel
SURFACE AREA	How many sticky notes will cover the cabinet?	File Cabinet	Andrew Stadel

FIGURE 9.11

Conclusion

Modeling is not for mathematics only—it transcends disciplines and affords a powerful tool for students to engage with real problems in their future careers and in society. When used correctly, mathematical modeling encourages students to stop viewing mathematics as techniques and procedures and to start viewing it as a tool to solve problems (Biembengut and Hein 2010). W. Gary Martin, a professor of mathematics education at Auburn University, says it best: "We keep teaching that learning to carry out complicated procedures is what math is about. To me the real question is, can students do anything with it?" (Cavanagh 2009).

Guiding Questions

1. Why do you think that mathematical modeling is being so strongly advocated for by the National Council of Teachers of Mathematics and by the Common Core State Standards for Mathematics?

2. What are some reasons you could use to justify adding mathematical modeling tasks to your courses? What are some reasons why this would be difficult to do, and how might you and your colleagues overcome these obstacles?

3. After trying out some of the modeling tasks in this chapter, how and where could you embed such tasks into your existing curriculum?

Part 4

Implementation Guidance

U p to this point, we have provided a slew of ideas about why high school mathematics needs to change dramatically and a range of specific suggestions about what many of these changes might look like. We have also focused on "how" invigorated mathematics classrooms should look. It is finally time to turn to the broader questions of "Exactly how do we move toward these changes in a careful, thoughtful, and collaborative manner?" and "What specific resources are currently available to support these changes?"

Accordingly, Part 4 provides specific answers to both of these questions and reminds everyone that most new initiatives fail not because they are the wrong initiative, but because their implementation was sloppy, undersupported, poorly planned, and/or imposed without adequate time or leadership. Additionally, we identify a large set of resources because none of this work entails reinventing the wheel. An extraordinary wealth of resources exists—most available without cost on the internet—allowing teachers and curriculum developers to start with readily available courses, units, and lessons that can be adapted far more easily than created from scratch.

10

Ideas are useless unless used. The proof
of their value is in their implementation.
Until then, they are in limbo.

—THEODORE LEVITT (2002)

Implementation

*A Game Plan
for Moving Forward*

CONSIDER THE MAGNITUDE of what we believe it will take to truly invigorate high school mathematics so that it truly works for all students. Reflect on the scope of the changes and shifts we believe are necessary to create effective, equitable, and engaging programs of study. In the previous chapters, we asked that concerned and affected stakeholders carefully review the array of current challenges, critically reflect on the excuses used to maintain an underperforming status quo, and thoughtfully consider a set of guiding principles, as preparation for changes in curriculum, pedagogy, assessment, and the use of technology, as well as an increased focus on mathematical modeling. It is a no-brainer that this will take time and deliberate implementation.

Fortunately, there is much we know about educational change. Unfortunately, too often there is very little we do in schools that recognizes this knowledge about change. For example,

- Change takes time, but too often we are asked to implement changes prematurely, before getting buy-in and before those who need to do the implementation are adequately trained and ready.

- Change begins with informed discussion, but too often the scope of change is imposed without adequate discussion or without building a consensus for change.

- Change takes careful planning, but too often insufficient time and resources are allocated to this essential step, resulting in decisions that are imposed, made prematurely, or made without adequate thought to their implications.

- Change takes winning over colleagues and decision makers, but too often we ignore recalcitrant colleagues who undermine change initiatives, we leave administrators having to defend decisions they don't understand, and we forget that board members will worry that changes will negatively affect their own, or their neighbor's, children, and we fail to brief all decision makers early in the process and continuously over time.

- Change requires mutual trust, a sense of collegiality, and shared purpose that must be built, but too often failure is blamed on recalcitrant teachers who are left uninvolved or uncommitted to the change.

- Change requires support, but too often the time, resources, and outside consultative assistance are not forthcoming.

- Change requires careful monitoring, nimble revision, and ongoing refinement, but too often change is "one and done," without a deep understanding that nothing of quality is done in one iteration.

It is therefore a certainty that high school mathematics will not be invigorated without careful attention to what we know about change in educational settings.

Phases and Conditions of Effective Change

Michael Fullan (n.d.), the guru of effective change and implementation in school settings, argues, on the basis of years of study, that there are four clear and distinct phases to the change process.

1. There must be a shared understanding and acknowledgment that problems and/or needs exist and must be solved.

2. There must be evidence-based, consensus-driven initial planning.

3. There must be a process of iterative implementation with close monitoring, review, and revision.

4. There is finally the institutionalization of changes.

Let's parse out these four phases one by one to ensure that everyone involved in the process understands its complexity and the range of necessary conditions for embarking on and successfully implementing this work.

A shared understanding and acknowledgment that problems and needs exist. No change initiative is going anywhere if those charged with making the changes—in this case, high school mathematics teachers—don't believe that these changes are necessary, that they can be accomplished, and that adequate time and support will be available. We all need to understand up front the common experience that teachers have with top-down directives and mandates for which little more is provided than a new textbook that arrives a month before the start of the new school year. We need to understand that school and district administrators not only must tangibly support this process, but also must be ready to give teachers permission to take risks and must provide a safe space when teachers face the inevitable complaints from parents uninterested in any change that fails to privilege their own children.

That is why the critical first step, long before people start worrying about implementation, is securing broad agreement that there are real needs that are not being met and critical problems that need to be solved. This entails a stimulating, challenging, and often frustrating year of study. We urge teachers and administrators to collaborate on "book studies" of resources like this book or NCTM's *Catalyzing Change in High School Mathematics* (2018), as well as some of the reports listed in Chapter 11. We hope that this year of analysis results in such documents and activities as

- a statement of current conditions, including courses, enrollments, report card grade distributions, disaggregated achievement data, professional development opportunities, status and quality of course assessments, and student support mechanisms

- the identification of needs and problems as well as obstacles to change based on a comparison of current conditions and the recommendations that emerge from the "book study" resources

- a series of department retreats to build consensus on areas of relative strength, relative weakness, and initial focus

- documentation, in a shared folder, of all written summaries.

Teachers who have engaged in such a yearlong process of building a shared understanding of common problems and potential solutions report that this work constitutes some of the most powerful professional growth of their careers.

Initial planning. As Fullan argues, the careful development of a shared understanding and acknowledgment that problems and/or needs exist is both a natural and essential precursor to planning. That is, initial planning involves answering the questions "Where can we start?" and "Who will be doing what, when, and with what time frame, collaboration, support, and guidance?" Effective planning mitigates against the all-too-common "I don't know why we're doing these things or even how to begin" that so easily undermines motivation and commitment to change. That is why it is particularly important that all meetings are organized around a previously distributed agenda and premeeting assignments when appropriate. Little saps energy and motivation more efficiently than wasted time and unfocused meetings.

In addition to recognizing that planning requires focused time commitments and cannot be done by a single person working alone, effective planning most often requires the following elements:

- a clear understanding that planning, like implementation, is an iterative process that involves continual review and revision, meaning that initial decisions are viewed as only tentative and subject to ongoing review and reconsideration

- a process to keep all stakeholders involved in, and aware of, the emerging plans

- communication and transparency so no one is given an opportunity to feel sandbagged

- the identification of potential instructional resources for each course

- reliance on outside experts, critical friends, and coaches.

Iterative implementation. Nothing works right the first time. No matter how careful the planning, glitches emerge, mistakes get made, and initial judgments prove faulty, requiring a broadly shared understanding that high-quality, sustainable change emerges only from an iterative process of trial, monitoring and review, and revision and retrial. Nowhere in the process is transparency and open and honest discussion more important than at the stage of initial and iterative implementation, lesson by lesson, unit by unit, and course by course. As Fullan (2001b) notes, the logic behind the implementation of change at the department and district levels should be clear—"no matter how promising a new idea may be, it cannot impact student learning if it is superficially implemented."

Two to three years of iterative implementation requires an abiding mindset that essentially nothing of quality is accomplished on the first try. It requires a shared process of monitoring, which is why formative assessments and common, aligned, high-quality summative unit assessments are so important from the very start. It requires a respect for those who are doing the implementation. And it requires the active and meaningful engagement of the entire mathematics department.

Institutionalization. Effective implementation of changes of the magnitude proposed for high school mathematics cannot be done overnight or without careful planning. Moreover, what has been proposed in this book requires the understanding that actual institutionalization is unlikely to occur anytime sooner than the fifth year of work. As we have noted, we have spent over one hundred years making little more than tiny shifts to get to where we are. It is unlikely that we can break such an institutionalized pattern in anything less than five years of intense work. However, when there is broad agreement that change is nonnegotiable and planning includes a genuine investment in meaningful planning and iterative implementation, it is reasonable to believe that during year five, we can all begin to take real pride in an invigorated high school mathematics program! And then, of course, because nothing stays the same, the entire process begins again.

A Five-Year Proposed Plan for Invigorating High School Math

Building from these elements and conditions for effectively carrying out a change process, we propose a five-year approach for consideration and adaptation wherein

- Year 1 is a year of study and building an emerging consensus.

- Year 2 is a year of initial implementation and intense planning.

- Years 3 and 4 are years of implementation, monitoring, and revision, with intensive evaluation of impact in Year 4.

- Year 5 is a year of institutionalization.

For year-by-year descriptions of the five-year approach, see Figures 10.1 to 10.5.

YEAR 1: REVIEW CURRENT CONDITIONS, READ RESEARCH, AND BUILD CONSENSUS

FOCUS	SUGGESTED ACTIVITIES	PRODUCTS

▪ Analysis of current conditions
▪ Review of relevant literature
▪ Building consensus on where and how to begin
	▪ Have the entire department read Chapter 3 of this book; individually and collectively respond to "Questions to Ask Yourselves."
	▪ Conduct a book study of NCTM's *Catalyzing Change in High School Mathematics* (2018) and other reports listed in Chapter 11.
	▪ Establish time for department-wide professional learning communities and begin to build collaborative structures such as collegial classroom visits and lesson videotaping reviews.
	▪ Conduct a one-day department retreat to build consensus on
	  ▪ areas of relative strength
	  ▪ areas of relative weakness
	  ▪ areas to focus on first.
	▪ Identify initial targets of change, for example, increasing instructional time, instituting the grades 9 and 10 integrated courses, strengthening unit assessments, identifying instructional resources, using technology more effectively, and/or strengthening the department's professional culture.
	▪ Develop and agree on a plan for initial implementation of Year 2 shifts and unit-level pilots of changes.
		▪ Summaries of findings, discussions, strengths, and weaknesses
		▪ Draft of the plan for Year 2

FIGURE 10.1

YEAR 2: PILOT OF VARIOUS SHIFTS		
FOCUS	**SUGGESTED ACTIVITIES**	**PRODUCTS**
• Initial implementation of shifts in pedagogy, assessment, technology, and the use of available resources • Planning for shifts in curriculum	• Institutionalize professional learning community sessions, collegial classroom visits, and videotaping analysis to strengthen the department's culture of collaboration. • Establish course/pathway committees to begin the process of fleshing out course goals, course units and topics, and learning expectations for each unit and begin to identify potential instructional resources for new courses for grades 9 (Integrated High School Mathematics 1) and 11 (one course selected from Chapter 5). • Provide coaching and support in the areas of shifting pedagogical practices, assessment practices, and technology usage in all existing courses. • Provide administrators and guidance counselors with periodic updates on developing plans and the draft of the language for the following year's course catalogs. • Identify and deploy outside experts, consultants, and critical friends as needed. • Develop and agree on a plan for Year 3 initial implementation of new courses.	• Summaries of findings, discussions, strengths, and weaknesses • End-of-year summary of expected challenges • Language for the new courses for grades 9 and 11 for the school's course catalog • Draft of the plan for Year 3 • Report to the school board on progress toward invigorating high school mathematics

FIGURE 10.2

YEAR 3: INITIAL IMPLEMENTATION OF TWO NEW COURSES

FOCUS	SUGGESTED ACTIVITIES	PRODUCTS
<ul><li>Initial implementation of new courses in grades 9 (Integrated High School Mathematics 1) and 11 (one course selected from Chapter 5)</li><li>Continued attention to shifts in pedagogy, assessment, technology, and the use of available resources</li><li>Monitoring and revision of implementation</li></ul>	<ul><li>Monitor, via lesson plans, collegial observations and debriefing discussions, videos of selected lessons, and student artifacts, the success of initial implementation of new courses.</li><li>Establish course/pathway committees to continue the process of fleshing out course goals, course units and topics, and learning expectations for each unit and begin to identify potential instructional resources for a new course for grade 10 (Integrated High School Mathematics 2), additional alternatives in grade 11, and selection of courses for grade 12.</li><li>Continue to deploy outside experts, consultants, and critical friends as needed.</li><li>Develop and agree on a plan for Year 4 initial implementation of new courses.</li></ul>	<ul><li>Summary of what has worked, what has been problematic, and strategies for overcoming these problems</li><li>Specific unit-by-unit report on proposed changes in time allocations, learning expectations, resources, and activities</li><li>Draft of the plan for Year 4</li><li>Report to the school board on progress toward invigorating high school mathematics</li></ul>

FIGURE 10.3

YEAR 4: IMPLEMENTATION OF MORE COURSES

FOCUS	SUGGESTED ACTIVITIES	PRODUCTS
<ul><li>Second iteration of new courses—Integrated High School Mathematics 1 in grade 9 and one course selected in grade 11</li><li>Initial implementation of new courses—Integrated High School Mathematics 2 in grade 10, an additional alternative in grade 11, and one course in grade 12</li><li>Continued attention to shifts in pedagogy, assessment, technology, and the use of available resources</li><li>Monitoring and revision of implementation</li><li>Intensive evaluation of changes and impact</li></ul>	<ul><li>Carefully monitor and debug the second iteration of new courses—Integrated High School Mathematics 1 in grade 9 and one course in grade 11—with particular attention to remaining problems and weaknesses.</li><li>Monitor, via lesson plans, collegial observations and debriefing discussions, videos of selected lessons, and student artifacts, the success of initial implementation for the course for grade 10 (Integrated High School Mathematics 2), additional alternatives in grade 11, and one course in grade 12.</li><li>Continue to deploy outside experts, consultants, and critical friends as needed.</li><li>Develop and agree on a plan for Year 5 full implementation.</li></ul>	<ul><li>Summary of what has worked, what has been problematic, and strategies for overcoming these problems</li><li>Specific unit-by-unit report on proposed changes in time allocations, learning expectations, resources, and activities</li><li>Draft of the plan for Year 5</li><li>Report to the school board on progress toward invigorating high school mathematics</li></ul>

FIGURE 10.4

YEAR 5: INSTITUTIONALIZATION		
FOCUS	**SUGGESTED ACTIVITIES**	**PRODUCTS**
▪ Institution-alization of invigorated high school mathematics program	▪ Carefully monitor and debug the second iteration of new courses—Integrated High School Mathematics 2 in grade 10, additional alternatives in grade 11, and one course in grade 12—with particular attention to remaining problems and weaknesses. ▪ Focus on institutionalizing support for teachers to sustain these changes. ▪ Continue to monitor and make necessary (and hopefully minor) revisions. ▪ Maintain professional and collaborative structures.	▪ A well-deserved celebration!

FIGURE 10.5

Conclusion

We began this chapter with a list of seven bullet points, each in the form of "Change requires . . . but too often . . ." Our experiences are that in far too many situations, the "but too oftens" prevail and little sustainable change takes root. We tried to identify some of the reasons for this so they can perhaps be avoided or overcome. We tried to suggest specific elements for each of four research-affirmed phases of the change process. And we tried to propose a detailed five-year plan that enhances the odds of successful implementation of the range of changes that invigorate high school mathematics.

But we would be irresponsible if we fell into the trap of believing we have provided all the answers you and your colleagues will need or if we left you believing that this work will be easy. Instead, we hope that in this book and this chapter we have provided a slew of ideas and an outline of an implementation plan upon which to build. In addition, we have acknowledged that this is *hard* work. Hard work that will take time, study, trial and error, and a determination to overcome years of tradition and a range of unexpected obstacles, but hard work that can, and must, be accomplished over time, collaboratively and for the betterment of our students.

Guiding Questions

1. When thinking about implementation, what are your greatest fears or concerns about what might undermine the process?

2. What support and conditions do you believe would be necessary to carry out an effective implementation process?

3. Which aspects of Figure 10.1 are most in need of careful thought in your school or setting?

11

Resources

Great Places to Begin

GREAT! So we have acknowledged challenges, guiding principles, course units and essential topics, structures for differentiated pathways, and a slew of guidance on pedagogy, assessment, technology, modeling, and implementation. But the dominant questions are

- If I don't have a textbook, where do I find core, aligned, and powerful resources upon which to build coherent courses?

- Where can I find additional support and justification for these changes?

The good news is that answers to these questions already exist and are readily available in a broad array of free, online, high-quality resources that can be cherry-picked to support every one of the units of high school mathematics suggested in this book. Figures 11.1 to 11.7 list the available resources that we urge teachers and curriculum developers to start with. To access all links in one place, go to https://tinyurl.com/MilouLeinwand.

GRADES 9 AND 10 RESOURCES

WEBSITE	URL	DESCRIPTION
Illustrative Math High School Mathematics	https://illustrativemathematics.org/math-curriculum/9-12-math/?gclid=Cj0KCQjw8vqGBhC_ARIsADMSd1DmMrjr3JPo2qX-PgCdWwmjFvD7B38PaYeqx-qaTZOyVpqnOcTfxR7SMaAh-czEALw_wcB	A complete, online three-year Algebra 1, Geometry, and Algebra 2 program.
Mathematics Vision Project	www.mathematicsvisionproject.org	A complete, online three-year Integrated High School Mathematics program.
YouCubed	www.youcubed.org	A website that has inspirational math ideas and research on math mindset by Jo Boaler.
San Francisco Unified School District Math Curriculum	www.sfusdmath.org	Some of the best ideas and resources for detracking high school mathematics.

FIGURE 11.1

GRADES 11 AND 12 RESOURCES (INCLUDING STATISTICS AND DATA SCIENCE)

WEBSITE	URL	DESCRIPTION
Introduction to Data Science Curriculum	www.introdatascience.org	A curriculum for Introduction to Data Science (IDS), which teaches students to reason with, and think critically about, data in all forms.
Quantitative Reasoning Curriculum	www.utdanacenter.org /our-work/higher-education/higher -education-curricular-resources /quantitative-reasoning	A modern course featuring quantitative reasoning topics grounded in real-world contexts.
Dana Center Math Pathways	www.utdanacenter.org/our-work /higher-education/dana-center -mathematics-pathways	A website dedicated to modernizing American mathematics with equitable pathways for student success.
State of Oregon High School Core Math Guidance	www.oregon.gov/ode/educator -resources/standards/mathematics /Documents/High%20School%20 Core%20Mathematics%20 Guidance.pdf	A new course pathway model with two credits of core content for all students, with third-credit pathway options that align to student interests and goals. This model is referred to as the 2+1 course model.
Stats Medic	www.statsmedic.com	Detailed and comprehensive lesson plans for statistics and AP Statistics teachers to lead student-centered classrooms.
Skew the Script	https://skewthescript.org /ap-stats-curriculum?s=09	A curriculum that explores relevant data in social issues, economics, politics, medicine, sports, and more.
Mathematics Vision Project	www.mathematicsvisionproject.org	A complete, online three-year Integrated High School Mathematics program.
Illustrative Math High School Mathematics	https://illustrativemathematics.org /math-curriculum/9-12-math /?gclid=Cj0KCQjw8vqGBhC _ARIsADMSd1DmMrjr3JPo2qXPgC- dWwmjFvD7B38PaYeqxqaTZOyVpq- nOcTfxR7SMaAhczEALw_wcB	A complete, online three-year Algebra 1, Geometry, and Algebra 2 program.

FIGURE 11.2

ASSESSMENT RESOURCES

WEBSITE	URL	DESCRIPTION
Open Middle	www.openmiddle.com	Open Middle problems generally require a higher DoK than most problems that assess procedural and conceptual understanding. They provide students with opportunities for discussing their thinking.
Open Middle Problems in Google Slides	https://docs.google.com/document/d/1vqdixEiccYJhe8LcDilyNmtlmZbsG9Nd_jR8TgRFonA/edit	
Open Middle Problems in Desmos	https://teacher.desmos.com/collection/5d5c7cdd2eafb146f4614030	
Play with your Math	https://playwithyourmath.com	The site adapts math problems into interactive games. Also includes posters and handouts that hook students visually and explain the problem in just enough words.
Menu Math	http://natbanting.com/menu-math	Menu Math (Nat Banting) is a collection of constraints that appear as unordered lists, generally about six to ten constraints long. Each menu prescribes a type of mathematical object that needs to be designed to satisfy these constraints.
Balanced Assessment	https://hgse.balancedassessment.org	The project developed a large collection of innovative mathematics assessment tasks for grades K–12 and trained teachers to use these assessments in their classrooms.
Mathematics Assessment Project	www.map.mathshell.org/index.php	The project designed and developed well-engineered tools for formative and summative assessment that expose students' mathematical knowledge and reasoning, helping teachers guide them toward improvement and monitor progress.
Inside Mathematics	www.insidemathematics.org	A professional resource for teachers, coaches, and administrators who seek to improve students' mathematics learning and performance.

FIGURE 11.3

TECHNOLOGY RESOURCES

WEBSITE	URL	DESCRIPTION
Desmos Activities	https://docs.google.com /spreadsheets/d/1NUxX-yD89 gbCGmC_qb5rzugD9ebXL5n X65cR-1s5nRAedit#gid= 1038106211	A large collection of Desmos activities.
Flipgrid	https://info.flipgrid.com	A site that allows students to record and share short videos on any topic.
EdPuzzle	https://edpuzzle.com	A site that allows you to create interactive video lessons that you can integrate with embedded questions.
Pear Deck	www.peardeck.com	A Google-based app for active learning and formative assessment with takeaways.
Gimkit	www.gimkit.com	A game show for the classroom that requires knowledge, collaboration, and strategy to win.
Edulastic	https://edulastic.com	Online assessment tools with technology-enhanced items that give you a complete, instant view of student learning.
MathTV	www.mathtv.com	Over ten thousand videos covering topics from basic mathematics to calculus, with the problem given up front.
ClassKick	https://classkick.com	An app that allows you to see all your students work and give high-quality feedback from anywhere.
DeltaMath	www.deltamath.com	Review courses for students with instructional videos and access to over one thousand different skills.
Graspable Math	https://graspablemath.com	Activities in which students move terms fluently with their mouse or touch screen to solve equations and explore the power of algebra without frustration.
CanFigureIt	www.canfigureit.com	A unique way to visualize, learn, and teach geometric proofs using technology.

FIGURE 11.4

MODELING RESOURCES		
WEBSITE	**URL**	**DESCRIPTION**
Guidelines for Assessment and Instruction in Mathematical Modeling Education	www.siam.org/Portals/0/Publications /Reports/gaimme-full_color_for_online _viewing.pdf?ver=2018-03-19-115454-057	In 2015, leaders from SIAM and COMAP came together to produce this report.
Mathematical Modeling Handbook	www.comap.com/modelingHB /Modeling_HB_Sample.pdf	The "Teachers College Mathematical Modeling Handbook" is intended to support the implementation of the high school mathematical modeling conceptual category.
Emergent Math	https://emergentmath.com	This site is dedicated to problem-based curriculum maps for grades 3 to 11.
Three-Act Tasks (Dan Meyer)	https://docs.google.com/spreadsheets/d /1jXSt_CoDzyDFeJimZxnhgwOVsWkTQE sfqouLWNNC6Z4/edit#gid=0	A three-act task is a whole-group mathematics task consisting of three distinct parts: an engaging and perplexing Act 1, an information- and solution-seeking Act 2, and a solution-discussing and solution-revealing Act 3 (see Chapter 9).
Three-Act Tasks (Andrew Stadel)	https://docs.google.com/spreadsheets/d /19sms4MpuAOO71o4qFPJyVKK -OGLnNegMgSL6WAwldb8/edit#gid=0	
Three-Act Tasks (Robert Kaplinsky)	http://robertkaplinsky.com/lessons	
Three-Act Tasks (Kyle Pearce)	https://tapintoteenminds.com/3act-math	
Citizen Math	www.citizenmath.com	The site, formerly Mathalicious, offers real-world lessons that challenge students to think critically about the world.

FIGURE 11.5

OTHER RESOURCES

WEBSITE	URL	DESCRIPTION
Estimation 180	https://estimation180.com	Math lessons by Andrew Stadel that build number sense.
SolveMe Puzzles	https://solveme.edc.org	A broad array of algebraic thinking puzzles.
Visual Patterns	www.visualpatterns.org	An amazing array from Fawn Nguyen, perfect for algebraic thinking.
Which One Doesn't Belong?	http://wodb.ca	Thought-provoking puzzles by Mary Bourassa for math teachers and students alike. There are no answers provided, as there are many different, correct ways of choosing which one doesn't belong.
Would You Rather?	www.wouldyourathermath.com	Activities by John Stevens that ask students to choose a path and justify it with math.
Always, Sometimes, Never	http://asnmath.blogspot.com/p/asn-slide-shows.html	Always, Sometimes, Never questions that challenge students to think critically about math.
Graphing Stories	www.graphingstories.com	Short, fifteen-second videos that help students see and make graphs of real events.
Slow Reveal Graphs	https://slowrevealgraphs.com	An instructional routine to promote sense making about data.

FIGURE 11.6

REPORTS FOR IDEAS AND BUILDING COMPELLING ARGUMENTS FOR CHANGE

REPORT NAME	URL
"Introducing GAISE II: A Guideline for Precollege Statistics and Data Science Education"	https://hdsr.mitpress.mit.edu/pub/cqncbp3l /release/4
Catalyzing Change in High School Mathematics (NCTM)	www.nctm.org/change
Principles to Actions (NCTM)	www.nctm.org/Store/Products/Principles-to-Actions –Ensuring-Mathematical-Success-for-All
A Common Vision for Undergraduate Mathematical Sciences Programs in 2025 (MAA)	www.maa.org/sites/default/files/pdf/common-vision /common_vision_draft.pdf
"Branching Out: Designing Math Pathways for Equity"	https://justequations.org/resource/branching-out -designing-high-school-math-pathways-for-equity
Launch Years: A New Vision for the Transition from High School to Postsecondary Mathematics	www.utdanacenter.org/sites/default/files/2020-03 /Launch-Years-A-New-Vision-report-March-2020.pdf
NCTM Position Statements	www.nctm.org/Standards-and-Positions/NCTM -Position-Statements
"Insights from the MAA National Study of College Calculus"	https://drive.google.com/file/d/1AncZt90u37HwVy R6ACNnuSHYlDD8XXUz/view?usp=sharing
2018 National Survey of Science and Mathematics Education	http://horizon-research.com/NSSME
What Does It Really Mean to Be College and Work Ready? (NCEE)	http://ncee.org/wp-content/uploads/2013/05/NCEE _MathReport_May20131.pdf

FIGURE 11.7

Appendix

Innovations from the States

Oregon

The Oregon Department of Education has released its 2021 draft high school math standards, which can be found at www.oregon.gov/ode/educator-resources/standards /mathematics/Documents/Draft%20Math%20Standards/2021.01%20High%20School _Version%203.3%20(Accessible).pdf. The state has narrowed down the number of high school math standards from 147 to 55, with about half of those being algebra and the remaining half split between geometry and data/statistics (see Figure A.1).

High School Domain	Original Number of Standards (NGA Center and CCSSO 2010)	Number of Core Standards (Jan. 2021 Draft)	Advanced (+) Standards Removed (Jan. 2021 Draft)	Non-Advanced Standards Removed (Jan. 2021 Draft)	Proposed Merged Standards (Jan. 2021 Draft)
HS Algebra (HSA)	27	11	4	12	0
HS Functions (HSF)	28	10	7	11	0
HS Number (HSN)	27	4	18	5	0
HS Geometry	41	14	6	12	9
HS Data Science and Statistics (HSS)	24	16	2	6	0
Total Count	147	55	37	46	9

FIGURE A.1

The core content (first two years of high school) is balanced between approximately 1 credit of algebra content, $\frac{1}{2}$ credit of geometry, and $\frac{1}{2}$ credit of data science and statistics. For third-year options, Oregon high schools are invited to innovate by offering new specialized courses within three general paths: (1) a pathway to calculus, (2) a pathway to data science, and (3) a pathway to quantitative mathematics. Figure A.2 helps us visualize the long-term goal of what high school math pathways in the 2+1 model could look like.

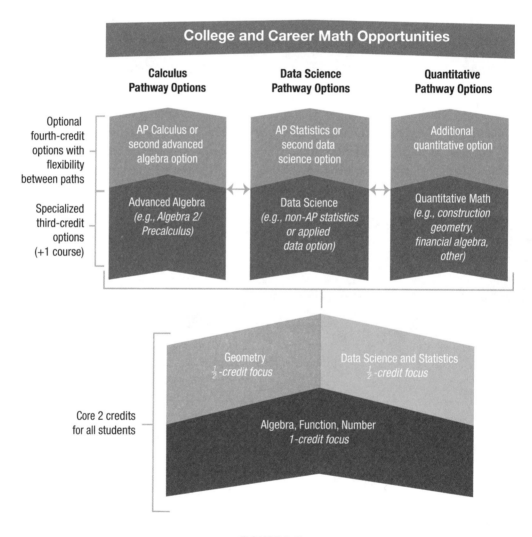

FIGURE A.2

Virginia

Taking an approach similar to Oregon's, the state of Virginia has created the Virginia Mathematics Pathways Initiative (VMPI), which is a joint initiative of the Virginia Department of Education (VDOE), the State Council of Higher Education for Virginia (SCHEV), and the Virginia Community College System (VCCS). The initiative creates mathematics pathways to address the knowledge, skills, experiences, and attributes that students must attain to be successful in college and/or the workforce. The pathways include two years of essential math concepts followed by $\frac{1}{2}$-credit and full-credit course options in grades 11 and 12. See more at www.doe.virginia.gov /instruction/mathematics/vmpi/index.shtml#vmpi.

California

In early 2021, the state of California released the 2021 revision of the California Mathematics Frameworks, which can be found at www.cde.ca.gov/ci/ma/cf/. The framework has thirteen chapters, including chapters on middle and high school (Chapters 7 and 8) and a data science chapter (Chapter 5) outlining an approach that enables all students to move to calculus, data science, statistics, or other high-level courses, with grade-level courses in grades 6, 7, and 8 in middle school. The new provision of a data science high school course that is open to all students and can serve as a replacement for Algebra 2 has the potential to open STEAM pathways to diverse groups of students, both through its engaging content and its openness to all students. Figure A.3 indicates possible pathways for high school coursework, reflecting a common ninth- and tenth-grade experience and a broader array of options in eleventh and twelfth grades. The figure indicates three pathways of courses for years one and two of high school and a cloud indicating a variety of course offerings for years three and four.

It should be noted that, in October 2020, the University of California (UC) system updated the mathematics course criteria and guidelines for the 2021–22 school year and beyond. The update includes the allowance of courses in data science to serve as the required third year of mathematics coursework. Mathematics: Investigating and Connecting (MIC)—Data Science meets the criteria and so fulfills the required third year. To see their framework, visit https://www.cde.ca.gov/ci/ma/cf/.

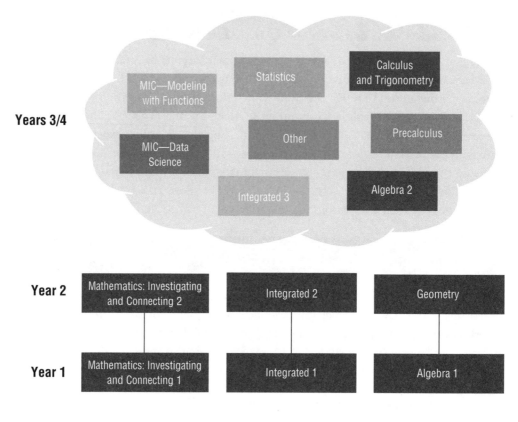

FIGURE A.3

Oklahoma

The state of Oklahoma has created an Algebra 1 course that we believe is exemplary and has narrowed the list of standards—eliminating most work on quadratics and exponential functions from Algebra 1. The units are listed below and details can be found at http://okmathframework.pbworks.com/w/browse/#view=ViewFolder&param=Algebra%20 1%20Units%20v2.

Unit 0: Math with a Growth Mindset

Unit 1: Expressions, Equations, and Inequalities

Unit 2: Data

Unit 3: Functions

Unit 4: Linear Functions

Unit 5: Systems

Unit 6: Probability

The full details of one unit (Unit 3: Functions) are shown in Figures A.4 to A.8.

ALGEBRA 1
Unit 3: Functions

Unit Driving Question

How can we use data to determine patterns and relationships in real-world situations?

Essential Questions

1. How do we measure change?
2. How do we quantify the relationships between quantities?
3. How can different representations show relationships?
4. What patterns exist among quantities?

LAUNCH TASK	BIG IDEAS FOR DEVELOPMENT LESSONS	CLOSURE AND ASSESSMENT
1 Lesson	**4 Weeks** (approximately 1 week per big idea)	**1 Week**
Students explore functions in 200 Freestyle	1. A function is a rule that describes the relationship in a set of data for which each input has one and only one output. 2. Functions are written and manipulated using function notation. 3. Functions can be evaluated and interpreted both algebraically and graphically. 4. Function families share similar graphs, behaviors, and properties.	1. Unit 3 Formative Assessment 1 2. Reengagement Activity (not provided, to be based on formative assessment results) 3. Tesla Performance Assessment (covers A1.F.1.2, A1.F.1.4, A1.A.4.1): For access to scoring rubric and student samples, complete the NextThought PLC Common Assessment Discussion, Implementation, and Analysis training module.

FIGURE A.4

BIG IDEA 1

A function is a rule that describes the relationship in a set of data for which each input has one and only one output.

OAS-M: A1.F.1.1, A1.F.1.2

Lessons and Additional Activities

Big Idea 1: Lesson Overview

- Lesson 1: Identify domain and range given in graph, table, mapping, and ordered pair form.
- Lesson 2: Know that relations are simply a mapping from the domain to the range and understand that functions are a well-mapped subdomain of a relation.
- Lesson 3: Identifying and Describing Relationships Between Variables
- Lesson 4: Connecting the Graph to the Situation and Justifying the Connection
- Lesson 5: Find restrictions to the domain and range when necessary.

Evidence of Understanding

Know that relations are simply a mapping from the domain to the range.

Understand that functions are a well-mapped subdomain of a relation.

- Realize that each element of the domain mapped to only one element in the range.

Identify domain and range of given function, equation, or graph.

- Domain is the set of *x*-coordinates within a set of points on a graph or within a written set of ordered pairs.
- These values are the input to a function or relation.
- Range is the set of *y*-coordinates within a set of points on a graph or within a written set of ordered pairs.
- These values are the output to a function or relation.

Identify independent and dependent variables of a given function, equation, or graph.

- Independent variables are the variable whose value determines the value of other variables.
- Dependent variables are the variable whose value is determined by the value of an independent variable.

Find restrictions to the domain and range when necessary.

- Understand that there are restrictions on domain and range in algebraic situations as well as real-world situations.
- Recognize when the domain or range may have values that do not exist in a real-world situation.

Interpret functions both verbally and graphically.

FIGURE A.5

BIG IDEA 2
Functions are written and manipulated using function notation.

OAS-M: A1.F.1.3, A1.F.3.3, A1.F.1.4

Lessons and Additional Activities

Big Idea 2: Lessons 1–4 Overview

Additional Collaborative Activity:

- Station Activity: Real-World Situation Graphs—Students will work in collaborative groups to complete station activities providing opportunities to develop concepts and skills related to creating and interpreting graphs representing real-world situations.

Evidence of Understanding

Understand what function notation represents in terms of the two variables and the relationship between them.

- Know that $f(x)$ is the dependent variable and x is the independent variable.
- Recognize how changing x changes $f(x)$.
- Understand $f(x) = mx + b$ is a linear function.

Understand rate of change in real-world situations is the slope of a function and initial value is the y-intercept.

Perform arithmetic operations on functions.

- Add and subtract functions in function notation.
- Multiply functions in function notation.

FIGURE A.6

BIG IDEA 3
Functions can be evaluated and interpreted both algebraically and graphically.

OAS-M: A1.F.1.3, A1.F.3.3

Lessons and Additional Activities	**Evidence of Understanding**
Big Idea 3: Lessons 1–2 Overview	*Recognize piecewise functions as a combination of equations.* ▪ Linear piecewise functions are formed by linear segments that correspond to a specific part of the domain. *Evaluate a function and interpret meaning in real-world situations both algebraically and graphically.*

FIGURE A.7

BIG IDEA 4
Function families share similar graphs, behaviors, and properties.

OAS-M: A1.F.2.1, A1.F.2.2, A1.A.3.6

Lessons and Additional Activities

Lesson Plans and Activities:

Big Idea 4: Lessons 1–4B Overview

Additional Collaborative Activities:

- Station Activity: Relations vs. Functions and Linear vs. Non-linear—Students will work in collaborative groups and complete station activities providing opportunities for students to develop concepts and skills related to recognizing the differences between linear and nonlinear functions and the differences between functions and relations.

- Pandemic: How do viruses spread through a population? (Mathalicious) In this lesson, students use exponential growth and logarithms to model how a virus spreads through a population and evaluate how various factors influence the speed and scope of an outbreak.

Evidence of Understanding

Recognize linear and nonlinear functions from tables, graphs, and equations.

- Realize linear functions change by equal intervals while exponential functions increase by equal factors over equal intervals.

Identify similarities and differences among linear, quadratic, absolute value, and exponential function families based on features of their graphs or tables.

- Interpret rate of change, domain and range patterns, and intercepts for each type of function family.

- Relate the rate of change and other key features of each function family to its parent function: $f(x) = x$ (linear), $f(x) = x^2$ (quadratic), $f(x) = |x|$ (absolute value), and $f(x) = 2^x$ (exponential).

Compare functions within a family and describe transformations from the parent function.

- Describe the vertical or horizontal shift given a graphical representation of a parent function and other function in the same family.

- Compare tables of values for different functions within the same function family (the parent function and one other).

Identify geometric sequences as exponential functions: $f(x) = a(r)^x$

- Define a and r within the context of the problem.

- Create various models of the given data, including equations, graphs, tables, and verbal descriptions.

- Find the next term in the sequence when given the formula.

Understand that an arithmetic sequence is a linear function and changes by adding (or subtracting) the same value each time.

- Be able to recognize an arithmetic sequence and write a rule to describe it using the formula.

- Use the rule to find the nth term in the sequence.

FIGURE A.8

Alabama

In the state of Alabama, we draw the reader to two innovative high school courses and call attention to starting high school math with Geometry with Data Analysis (Alabama State Department of Education 2019):

> Geometry with Data Analysis builds on students' experiences in the middle grades. It is the first required course in high school mathematics, providing a common grade 9 experience for all students entering high school–level mathematics.

> - Geometry with Data Analysis builds essential concepts necessary for students to meet their postsecondary goals (whether they pursue additional study or enter the workforce), to function as effective citizens, and to recognize the wonder, joy, and beauty of mathematics (NCTM 2018). It is important because it develops mathematical knowledge and skills through visual representations prior to the more abstract development of algebra.

> - Beginning high school mathematics with Geometry with Data Analysis in grade 9 offers students the opportunity to build their reasoning and sense-making skills, see the applicability of mathematics, and prepare more effectively for further studies in algebra. The course also focuses on data analysis, which provides students with tools to describe, show, and summarize data in the world around them.

> - In Geometry with Data Analysis, students incorporate knowledge and skills from several mathematics content areas, leading to a deeper understanding of fundamental relationships within the discipline and building a solid foundation for further study. In the content area of Geometry and Measurement, students build on and deepen prior understanding of transformations, congruence, similarity, and coordinate geometry concepts. Informal explorations of transformations provide a foundation for more formal considerations of congruence and similarity, including development of criteria for triangle congruence and similarity. An emphasis on reasoning and proof throughout the content area promotes exploration, conjecture testing, and informal and formal justification. Students extend their middle school work with conjecturing and creating informal arguments to more formal proofs in this course. (117)

Mathematical Modeling is a newly designed, specialized mathematics course developed to expand on and reinforce the concepts introduced in Geometry with Data Analysis, Algebra 1 with Probability, and Algebra 2 with Statistics by applying them in the context of mathematical modeling to represent and analyze data and make predictions regarding real-world phenomena.

- Mathematical Modeling is designed to engage students in doing, thinking about, and discussing mathematics, statistics, and modeling in everyday life. It allows students to experience mathematics and its applications in a variety of ways that promote financial literacy and data-based decision-making skills. This course also provides a solid foundation for students who are entering a range of fields involving quantitative reasoning, whether or not they require calculus. In this course, students explore decision-making for financial planning and management, designing in three dimensions, interpreting statistical studies, and creating functions to model change in the environment and society. Measurements are taken from the real world, and technology is used extensively for computation, with an emphasis on students' interpretation and explanation of results in context. Students will develop and use both the Mathematical Modeling Cycle and the Statistical Problem-Solving Cycle in this specialized course to further develop authentic decision-making skills. (149)

More details on these courses are available at www.alsde.edu/sec/sct /COS/2019%20Alabama%20Course%20of%20Study%20Mathematics.pdf.

References

Achieve. 2020. "The Algebra II Variable: State Policies for Graduation Requirements, Assessments, and Alignment to Postsecondary Expectations." www.achieve.org /files/Achieve_StateMathematicsPolicyLandscape_FINAL.pdf.

Aguirre, Julia Maria, Karen Mayfield-Ingram, and Danny Bernard Martin. 2013. *The Impact of Identity in K–8 Mathematics Learning and Teaching: Rethinking Equity-Based Practices*. Reston, VA: National Council of Teachers of Mathematics.

Alabama State Department of Education. 2019. *Alabama Course of Study: Mathematics*. www.alsde.edu/sec/sct/COS/2019%20Alabama%20Course%20of%20Study%20 Mathematics.pdf.

Allensworth, Elaine, and Kallie Clark. 2020. "High School GPAs and ACT Scores as Predictors of College Completion: Examining Assumptions About Consistency Across High Schools." *Educational Researcher* 49 (3): 198–211.

American Mathematical Association of Two-Year Colleges (AMATYC). 2014. "Position on the Appropriate Use of Intermediate Algebra as a Prerequisite Course." https://amatyc.org/page/PositionInterAlg.

Arnold, Stephen. n.d. "Making Algebra Meaningful with Technology." https://compasstech.com.au/MeaningfulAlgebra/index.html.

Banilower, Eric R., et al. 2006. "Lessons from a Decade of Mathematics and Science Reform: A Capstone Report for the Local Systemic Change Through Teacher Enhancement Initiative." Chapel Hill, NC: Horizon Research.

Berry, Robert Q., III. 2016. "Informing Teachers About Identities and Agency: Using the Stories of Black Middle School Boys Who Are Successful with School Mathematics." In *More Lessons Learned from Research: Helping All Students Understand Important Mathematics*, vol. 2, edited by Edward Silver and Patricia Anne Kenney, 25–37. Reston, VA: National Council of Teachers of Mathematics.

Biembengut, Maria, and Nelson Hein. 2010. "Mathematical Modeling: Implications for Teaching." DOI: 10.1007/978-1-4419-0561-1_41.

Bishop, Jessica Pierson. 2012. "'She's Always Been the Smart One. I've Always Been the Dumb One': Identities in the Mathematics Classroom." *Journal for Research in Mathematics Education* 43 (1): 34–74.

Black, Paul, et al. 2004. "Working Inside the Black Box: Assessment for Learning in the Classroom." *Phi Delta Kappan* 86 (1): 8–21.

Bliss, Karen, et al. 2016. *GAIMME: Guidelines for Assessment and Instruction in Mathematical Modeling Education*, edited by Sol Garfunkel and Michelle Montgomery. Philadelphia, PA: Consortium for Mathematics and Its Applications (COMAP) and Society for Industrial and Applied Mathematics (SIAM).

Boaler, Jo. 2018. "Data Science." YouCubed. www.youcubed.org/resource/data-literacy/.

———. 2019. "Opinion: Modern High School Math Should Be About Data Science—Not Algebra 2." *Los Angeles Times*, October 23. www.latimes.com/opinion/story/2019-10-23/math-high-school-algebra-data-statistics.

Bressoud, David. 2015. "Insights and Recommendations from the MAA National Study of College Calculus." *Mathematics Teacher* 109 (3): 178–85.

———. 2018. "Why Colleges Must Change How They Teach Calculus." World.edu, January 31. https://world.edu/colleges-must-change-teach-calculus/.

Burdman, Pamela. 2015. "Degrees of Freedom: Diversifying Math Requirements for College Readiness and Graduation." (Report 1 of a three-part series.) Stanford, CA: PACE: Policy Analysis for California Education and LearningWorks. www.edpolicyinca.org/publications/degrees-freedom-diversifying-math-requirements-college-readiness-and-graduation-report-1-3-part-series.

———. 2018. "A Quiet Revolt Reshaping the Pathway to College." EdSource, April 8. https://edsource.org/2018/a-quiet-revolt-reshaping-the-pathway-to-college/595712.

Burke, Michael 2021. "University of California Must Drop SAT, ACT Scores for Admissions and Scholarships." EdSource, May 15. https://edsource.org/2021/university-of-california-must-drop-sat-act-scores-for-admissions-and-scholarships/654842?utm_source=enl&utm_medium=eml&utm_campaign=EdBiz.

Cavanagh, Sean. 2009. "New Tack on Math Promoted." October 6. www.edweek.org/policy-politics/new-tack-on-math-promoted/2009/10.

Charles A. Dana Center at the University of Texas at Austin. 2016. *MyMathLab® for Quantitative Reasoning: Student In-Class Notebook*. Boston: Pearson.

———. 2018. "Co-requisite Courses: Narrowing the Gap Between Instruction and Supports." Dana Center Mathematics Pathways, July. https://dcmathpathways.org/sites/default/files/resources/2018-07/Co-req_Supports_2018_07_24.pdf.

———. 2020. "Launch Years: A New Vision for the Transition from High School to Postsecondary Mathematics." Austin, TX: Charles A. Dana Center at the University of Texas at Austin. https://utdanacenter.org/launchyears.

Danielson, Christopher, and Dan Meyer. 2016. "Increased Participation and Conversation Using Networked Devices." *Mathematics Teacher* 110 (4): 258–64.

Daro, Phil, and Harold Asturias. 2019. "Branching Out: Designing High School Math Pathways for Equity." Berkeley, CA: Just Equations. https://justequations.org/resource/branching-out-designing-high-school-math-pathways-for-equity/.

Datnow, Amanda, and Sam Stringfield. 2000. "Working Together for Reliable School Reform." *Journal of Education for Students Placed at Risk* 5 (1–2): 183–204.

Drijvers, Paul, Peter Boon, and Martin Van Reeuwijk. 2011. "Algebra and Technology." In *Secondary Algebra Education: Revisiting Topics and Themes and Exploring the Unknown*, edited by Paul Drijvers, 179–202. Rotterdam: Sense.

Einstein, Albert, and Leopold Infeld. 1938. *The Evolution of Physics*. New York: Simon & Schuster.

Fullan, Michael. 2001a. *The New Meaning of Educational Change*. 3rd ed. New York: Teachers College Press.

———. 2001b. *Leading in a Culture of Change*. San Francisco: Jossey-Bass.

———. 2003. "Implementing Change at the Building Level." In *Best Practices, Best Thinking, and Emerging Issues in School Leadership*, edited by William Owings and Leslie Kaplan. Thousand Oaks, CA: Corwin.

———. n.d. "Change Models." www.slideshare.net/sha_men17/fullan-change-model.

Georgetown University Center on Education and the Workforce. 2013. Calculations of O*NET 17.0 and American Community Survey data. Unpublished.

Gordon, Sheldon P. 2008. "What's Wrong with College Algebra?" *Primus* 18 (6): 516–41.

Gould, Robert, Suyen Moncada-Machado, Terri Johnson, and James Molyneux. 2015. *Introduction to Data Science Curriculum*. www.introdatascience.org/introduction-to-data-science-curriculum.

Hall, Doug. n.d. QuoteTab. www.quotetab.com/quote/by-doug-hall/dont-make-excuses-make-things-happen-make-changes-then-make-history.

Hatch, Thomas. 2000. "What Happens When Improvement Programs Collide?" Menlo Park, CA: Carnegie Foundation for the Advancement of Teaching.

Hattie, John. 2009. *Visible Learning*. New York: Routledge.

Hirsch, Christian, and James Fey. 2008. *Core-Plus Mathematics: Contemporary Mathematics in Context, Course 2*. New York: McGraw Hill.

Jensen, Eric. 2005. *Teaching with the Brain in Mind*. Alexandria, VA: Association for Supervision and Curriculum Development.

Jilk, Lisa M. 2014. "'Everybody Can Be Somebody:' Expanding and Valorizing Secondary School Mathematics Practices to Support Engagement and Success." In *Mathematics for Equity: A Framework for Successful Practice*, edited by Na'ilah S. Nasir, et al., 107–28. New York: Teachers College Press.

Kazemi, Elham, et al. 2016. "Listening to and Learning from Student Thinking." *Teaching Children Mathematics* 23 (3): 182–90.

Kennedy, John F. 1963. Address in the Assembly Hall at the Paulskirche in Frankfurt, June 26.

Kloosterman, Peter. 2010. "Mathematics Skills of 17-Year-Olds in the United States: 1978 to 2004." *Journal for Research in Mathematics Education* 41 (1): 20–51.

Larson, Matt. 2016. "President's Message: Bringing Needed Coherence and Focus to High School Mathematics." National Council of Teachers of Mathematics, October 25. www.nctm.org/News-and-Calendar/Messages-from-the-President/Archive/Matt-Larson/Bringing-Needed-Coherence-and-Focus-to-High-School-Mathematics.

Levitt, Theodore. 2002. "Creativity Is Not Enough." *Harvard Business Review*, August. https://hbr.org/2002/08/creativity-is-not-enough.

Mathematical Association of America (MAA). 2015. *2015 CUPM Curriculum Guide to Majors in the Mathematical Sciences*. Washington, DC: MAA.

Meyer, Dan. 2015. "Missing the Promise of Mathematical Modeling." *The Mathematics Teacher* 108 (8): 578–83.

Murrell, Peter C., Jr. 2007. *Race, Culture, and Schooling: Identities of Achievement in Multicultural Urban Schools*. Mahwah, NJ: Lawrence Erlbaum.

Nasir, Na'ilah Suad, and Victoria M. Hand. 2006. "Exploring Sociocultural Perspectives on Race, Culture, and Learning." *Review of Educational Research* 76 (4): 449–75.

National Center for Education Statistics (NCES). 2013. *The Nation's Report Card: Trends in Academic Progress, 2012*. Institute of Education Sciences, U.S. Department of Education: Washington, DC.

———. 2019. "Table 322.10. Bachelor's Degrees Conferred by Postsecondary Institutions, by Field of Study: Selected Years, 1970–71 Through 2016–17."

National Center on Education and the Economy (NCEE). 2013. "What Does It Really Mean to Be College and Work Ready? The Mathematics and English Literacy Required of First Year Community College Students." https://ncee.org/book-report/what-does-it-really-mean-to-be-college-and-work-ready.

National Commission on Excellence in Education. 1983. *A Nation at Risk: The Imperative for Educational Reform*. Washington, DC: The National Commission on Excellence in Education. www2.ed.gov/pubs/NatAtRisk/risk.html.

National Council of Teachers of Mathematics (NCTM). 1989. *Curriculum and Evaluation Standards for School Mathematics*. Reston, VA: NCTM.

———. 2000. *Principles and Standards for School Mathematics*. Reston, VA: NCTM.

———. 2014. *Principles to Actions: Ensuring Mathematical Success for All*. Reston, VA: NCTM.

———. 2015. "Strategic Use of Technology in Teaching and Learning Mathematics." www.nctm.org/Standards-and-Positions/Position-Statements/Strategic-Use-of-Technology-in-Teaching-and-Learning-Mathematics.

———. 2018. *Catalyzing Change in High School Mathematics: Initiating Critical Conversations*. Reston, VA: NCTM.

National Governors Association Center for Best Practices, Council of Chief State School Officers (NGA Center and CCSSO). 2010. *Common Core State Standards: Mathematics*. Washington, DC: National Governors Association Center for Best Practices, Council of Chief State School Officers.

National Mathematics Advisory Panel. 2008a. "The Final Report of the National Mathematics Advisory Panel." U.S. Department of Education.

———. 2008b. "Report of the Subcommittee on the National Survey of Algebra I Teachers." U.S. Department of Education.

Newmann, Fred, M. Bruce King, and Peter Youngs. 2001. "Professional Development That Addresses School Capacity: Lessons from Urban Elementary Schools." Paper presented at the annual meeting of AERA.

Oakes, Jeannie, et al. 1990. *Multiplying Inequalities: The Effects of Race, Social Class, and Tracking on Opportunities to Learn Mathematics and Science*. Santa Monica, CA: RAND.

Oppland-Cordell, Sarah, and Danny Bernard Martin. 2015. "Identity, Power, and Shifting Participation in a Mathematics Workshop: Latin@ Students' Negotiation of Self and Success." *Mathematics Education Research Journal* 27 (1): 21–49.

Pollak, Henry O. 2013. "What Is Mathematical Modeling?" Missouri Learning Standards. www.missourilearningstandards.com/files/cur-math-comcore-what-is-mathematical -modeling.pdf.

President's Council of Advisors on Science and Technology (PCAST). 2012. "Engage to Excel: Producing One Million Additional College Graduates with Degrees in Science, Technology, Engineering, and Mathematics." Washington, DC: White House Office of Science and Technology Policy. https://obamawhitehouse.archives. gov/sites/default/files/microsites/ostp/fact_sheet_final.pdf.

Rittle-Johnson, Bethany, Robert Siegler, and Martha W. Alibali. 2001. "Developing Conceptual Understanding and Procedural Skill in Mathematics: An Iterative Process." *Journal of Educational Psychology* 93 (2): 346–62.

Rutschow, Elizabeth Zachry. 2019. "The National Academies of Sciences, Engineering, and Medicine Workshop on Understanding Success and Failure of Students in Developmental Mathematics: Developmental Mathematics Reforms." Washington, DC: The National Academies of Sciences, Engineering, and Medicine. https:// sites.nationalacademies.org/cs/groups/dbassesite/documents/webpage /dbasse_191791.pdf.

Rutschow, Elizabeth Zachry, and John Diamond. 2015. "Laying the Foundations: Early Findings from the New Mathways Project." MDRC, April. www.mdrc.org/sites /default/files/New_Mathways_ES.pdf.

Saxe, Karen, and Linda Braddy. 2015. *A Common Vision for Undergraduate Mathematical Sciences Programs in 2025*. Washington, DC: Mathematical Association of America.

Schmidt, William H. 2009. "Exploring the Relationship Between Content Coverage and Achievement: Unpacking the Meaning of Tracking in Eighth Grade Mathematics." East Lansing, MI: The Education Policy Center at Michigan State University. http:// education.msu.edu/epc/forms/Schmidt_2009_Relationship_between_Content _Coverage_and_Achievement.pdf.

Schmidt, William H., Leland S. Cogan, and Curtis C. McKnight. 2010/2011. "Equality of Educational Opportunity: Myth or Reality in U.S. Schooling?" *American Educator* 34 (4) (Winter 2010/2011): 12–19.

Seeley, Cathy. 2019. "Is It Time to Kill Algebra 2?" National Council of Supervisor of Mathematics newsletter.

Steen, Lynn Arthur, ed. 1997. *Why Numbers Count: Quantitative Literacy for Tomorrow's America*. New York: College Entrance Examination Board.

Stiff, Lee V., and Janet L. Johnson. 2011. "Mathematical Reasoning and Sense Making Begins with the Opportunity to Learn." In *Focus in High School Mathematics: Fostering Reasoning and Sense Making for All Students*, edited by Marilyn E. Strutchens and Judith R. Quander, 85–100. Reston, VA: NCTM.

Strickland, Jonathan. 2013. "Statistically Speaking, Robot Vision Is Hard." FW:Thinking. www.fwthinking.com/blog/statistically-speaking-robot-vision-hard.

Tate, William F., and Celia Rousseau Anderson. 2002. "Access and Opportunity: The Political and Social Context of Mathematics Education." In *Handbook of International Research in Mathematics Education*, edited by Lyn D. English and David Kirshner, 271–300. Mahwah, NJ: Lawrence Erlbaum.

Webel, Corey, and Samuel Otten. 2015. "Teaching in a World with PhotoMath." *Mathematics Teacher* 109 (5): 368–73.

Weiss, Ira R., and Joan D. Pasley. 2004. "What Is High-Quality Instruction?" *Educational Leadership* 61 (5): 24–28.

Wiliam, Dylan, and Marnie Thompson. 2007. "Integrating Assessment with Instruction: What Will It Take to Make It Work?" In *The Future of Assessment: Shaping Teaching and Learning*, edited by Carol Anne Dwyer, 53–82. Mahwah, NJ: Lawrence Erlbaum.

Wolfram, Conrad. 2010. "Teaching Kids Real Math with Computers." TedGlobal, July. www.ted.com/talks/conrad_wolfram_teaching_kids_real_math_with_computers?language=en.

———. 2020. *The Math(s) Fix: An Education Blueprint for the AI Age*. Champaign, IL: Wolfram Media.

Figure 9.1: Reprinted with permission from *Mathematics Teacher*, copyright © 2015, by the National Council of Teachers of Mathematics. All rights reserved.

Pages 156–159; Figure 9.4; Figure 9.5; Figure 9.6: Adapted from "Charge!" by Michael Fenton from the author's website, Reason and Wonder. Reprinted by permission of the author.

Pages 160–161; Figure 9.10: Adapted from "Which Toilet Uses Less Water?" by Robert Kaplinsky from the author's self-titled website posted January 10, 2013. Reprinted by permission of the author.

Figures A.4–A.8: "Algebra 1 Unit 3: Functions Table," "Big Idea 1 Table," "Big Idea 2 Table," "Big Idea 3 Table," and "Big Idea 4 Table" from the OKMath Framework website. Reprinted by permission of the Oklahoma State Department of Education.